THE USBORNE
INTERNET-LINKED
CHILDREN'S
WORLD
ATLAS

Stephanie Turnbull and Emma Helbrough
Designers: Stephen Moncrieff and Andrea Slane
Consultant cartographic editor: Craig Asquith

Cartography by European Map Graphics Ltd
Map design by Laura Fearn and Keith Newell
Consultant: Dr. Roger Trend, Senior Lecturer in Earth Science
and Geography Education, University of Exeter

CONTENTS

Here you can see dramatic cloud formations at sunset over a desert in California, U.S.A. Below is a large sandstone arch, shaped by the weather over many years.

INTERNET LINKS

Throughout this book we have recommended websites where you can find out more about maps and places around the world.

To visit the sites, follow these simple steps to go to the **Usborne Quicklinks Website** where you will find links to take you to the websites:

1. Go to **www.usborne-quicklinks.com**
2. Type the keyword for this book: **atlas**
3. Type the page number of the link you want to visit.
4. Click on the links to go to the recommended sites.

When using the internet, make sure you follow the internet safety guidelines shown on the opposite page, and displayed on the Usborne Quicklinks Website.

Internet links

For links to all the websites described in this book, go to **www.usborne-quicklinks.com** and enter the keyword "atlas".

Help

For general help and advice on using the internet, go to the Usborne Quicklinks Website and click on "Net Help".

To find out more about using your web browser, click on your browser's Help menu and choose "Contents and Index". You'll find a searchable dictionary containing tips on how to find your way around the internet easily.

Here are some of the things you can do on the websites recommended in this book:
- Explore online maps of all the countries in the world.
- Take virtual tours of different countries, and listen to their languages.
- See satellite images of Earth's landforms, from the River Ganges to the Swiss Alps.
- Explore an Egyptian pyramid and go on a photo safari in Africa.
- Browse encyclopedia guides to the countries of the world.

Site availability

The links in Usborne Quicklinks are regularly reviewed and updated, but occasionally you may find a site is unavailable. This might be temporary, so try again later, or even the next day.

Websites do occasionally close down and when this happens, we will replace them with new links in Usborne Quicklinks. Sometimes we add extra links too, if we think they are useful, so when you visit Usborne Quicklinks, the links may be slightly different from those described in your book.

Computer not essential

If you don't have use of the internet, don't worry. This atlas is a complete, self-contained reference book on its own.

Extras

Some websites need additional programs, called plug-ins, to play sounds, or to show videos, animations or 3-D images. If you go to a site and you do not have the necessary plug-in, a message should come up on the screen.

There is usually a button on the site that you can click on to download the plug-in. Alternatively, go to Usborne Quicklinks and click on "Net Help". There you can find links to download plug-ins. Here is a list of plug-ins that you might need:

- **QuickTime** – lets you play video clips.

- **RealPlayer®** – lets you play video clips and sound files.

- **Flash™** – lets you play animations.

- **Shockwave®** – lets you play animations and enjoy interactive sites.

Computer viruses

A computer virus is a program that can damage your computer. A virus can get into your computer when you download programs from the internet, or in an attachment (an extra file) that arrives with an email. We strongly recommend that you buy anti-virus software to protect your computer and that you update the software regularly. You can buy anti-virus software at computer stores or download it from the internet. To find out more about viruses, go to Usborne Quicklinks and click on "Net Help".

Internet safety

When using the internet, make sure you follow these simple safety rules.
- Ask your parent's or guardian's permission before you connect to the internet. They can then stay nearby if they think they should do so.

- If you write a message in a website guest book, or on a website message board, do not include your email address, real name, address, phone number or the name of your school.

- If a website asks you to log in or register by typing your name or email address, ask the permission of an adult first.

- If you receive email from someone you don't know, tell an adult and do not reply to the email.

- Never arrange to meet anyone you have talked to on the internet.

Note for parents

The websites described in this book are regularly checked and reviewed by Usborne editors and the links in Usborne Quicklinks are updated. However, the content of a website may change at any time and Usborne Publishing is not responsible for the content of any website other than its own.

We recommend that children are supervised while on the internet, that they do not use internet chat rooms, and that you use internet filtering software to block unsuitable material. Please ensure that your children read and follow the safety guidelines above. For more information, go to the Net Help area on the Usborne Quicklinks Website at **www.usborne-quicklinks.com**

WHAT IS AN ATLAS?

An atlas is a collection of maps. This atlas helps you explore our world and find out more about its varied landscapes, famous cities and amazing sights.

What maps show

A map is an image that represents an area of the Earth's surface, usually from above. Unlike a photograph, which shows exactly what an area looks like, a map can show features of the area in a clear, simplified way. It can also give different information, such as place names. Symbols are often used to mark features such as volcanoes and waterfalls.

Which way is up?

Although the Earth doesn't have a top and a bottom, north is usually at the top of maps. But it is sometimes more convenient to reposition a map, so north might not necessarily be at the top. Some maps have a compass symbol that indicates where north lies.

Wolf volcano

Darwin volcano

San Salvador

Fernandina

Alcedo volcano

La Cumbre volcano

Isabela

Santa Cruz

Sierra Negra volcano

Cerro Azul volcano

This simple map of the central Galapagos Islands names the main islands and their volcanoes.

Floreana

This is a satellite image of part of the Galapagos Islands. Using the map on this page, can you identify the islands shown in the photograph?

Physical and political

Physical maps indicate natural features such as mountains, deserts, rivers and lakes. Political maps focus on the division of the Earth's surface into different countries. Look on pages 18–19 for a political map of the world, and on pages 20–21 for a physical map. Most of the maps in this atlas show physical features as well as country borders, cities and towns.

Map scales

The size of a map in relation to the area it shows is called its scale. Some maps have a scale bar, which is a rule with measurements. It tells you how many miles or km are represented by a certain distance on the map. Other maps show these relative distances just as numbers. For example, the figure 1:100 means that 1cm on the map represents 100cm on the Earth's surface.

The scale of a map depends on its purpose. A map showing the whole world is on a very small scale, but a town plan is on a much larger scale so that features such as roads can be shown clearly.

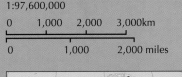

This map of Europe is on a small scale so that it all fits onto one small map.

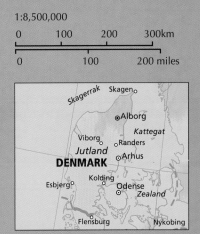

This map of Denmark is on a larger scale to show more detail.

Internet links

For links to the following websites, go to **www.usborne-quicklinks.com**

Website 1 Political maps of every country in the world, with helpful facts.

Website 2 An online guide to scale, with a test-yourself quiz.

This is Mount Rushmore, a huge sculpture of four U.S. presidents, which is one of the most famous sights in the U.S.A. Throughout this atlas you will see pictures of many more well known landmarks from around the world.

Using this atlas

The maps in this atlas are grouped by continent. There are seven continents, which are (from largest to smallest): Asia, Africa, North America, South America, Antarctica, Europe and Australasia and Oceania. Each map section is accompanied by photographs and satellite images showing some of the continent's most impressive sights. You can look up many of these places on the maps.

THE EARTH FROM SPACE

Modern technology has enabled scientists to make more accurate maps of the world than ever before. Even remote places, such as deserts, ocean floors and mountain ranges, have been mapped in detail, using information from satellites that observe the Earth from space.

What is a satellite?

Artificial satellites are machines that orbit, or travel around, the Earth. They observe the Earth using a technique called remote sensing. Instruments on the satellite monitor the Earth from a distance, and send back pictures of its surface. Satellites also monitor moons and other planets.

This satellite monitors the Earth 24 hours a day. It uses powerful radar that pierces through clouds. This means that the satellite can provide images of the Earth in all weather conditions.

Satellite movement

Some satellites orbit the Earth at a height of between 5km (3 miles) and 1,500km (930 miles), providing views of different parts of the planet. Others stay above the same place all the time, moving at the same speed as the Earth rotates to give a constant view of a particular area. These are called geostationary satellites. They travel at a height of around 36,000km (22,370 miles).

Internet links

For links to the following websites, go to **www.usborne-quicklinks.com**

Website 1 Look at detailed satellite pictures of any part of the world.
Website 2 Find out more about remote sensing and how satellites are used.
Website 3 How satellites monitor natural disasters, with a satellite jigsaw.

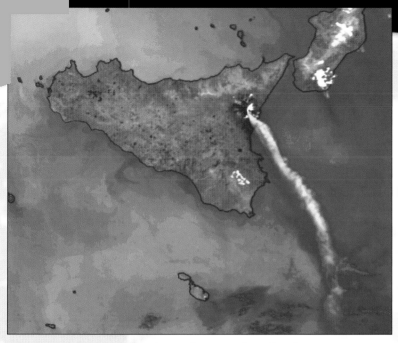

This satellite image of Sicily was taken in July 2001. It shows the volcano Mount Etna erupting. You can see smoke from the volcano on the right of the picture.

Satellite uses

Satellite pictures can be used to help predict and monitor natural hazards such as volcanic eruptions. They can also help scientists to observe the effects people have on the environment, for example the destruction of rainforests in South America. Satellite images are often artificially shaded to highlight relevant features, for example forests, so that they are easier to see.

Remote sensing

Satellites use a range of remote sensing techniques. One type is radar, which can provide images of the Earth even when it is dark or cloudy. Radar works by reflecting radio waves off a target object. The time it takes for a wave to bounce back indicates how far away the object is.

Powerful cameras provide pictures of the Earth's surface. Often, infrared cameras are used. Different surfaces reflect infrared rays differently, so infrared images of the Earth are able to show its various types of land surfaces, such as deserts, grasslands and forests.

This satellite image of the Earth is shaded to show different types of land. Deserts and other dry regions are red, and areas with lots of vegetation are orange.

DIVIDING LINES

The Earth is divided up with imaginary lines that help us measure distances and find where places are. There are two sets of lines, called latitude and longitude.

This arctic fox lives in northern Canada, very near the Arctic Circle line of latitude.

Latitude lines

Lines of latitude run around the globe. They are parallel to each other and get shorter the closer they are to the two poles. The latitude line that runs around the middle of the Earth is called the Equator. It is the most important line of latitude as all other lines are measured north or south of it.

Longitude lines

Lines of longitude run from the North Pole to the South Pole. All the lines are the same length, and they all meet at the North and South Poles.

The most important line of longitude is the Prime Meridian Line, which runs through Greenwich, in England. All other lines of longitude are measured east or west of this line.

Other lines

The Equator is not the only named line of latitude. The Tropic of Cancer is a line north of the Equator. The Tropic of Capricorn is at the same distance south of the Equator. Between these lines are the hottest, wettest parts of the world. This region is called the tropics.

The Arctic Circle is a latitude line far north of the Equator. The area north of this includes the North Pole and is called the Arctic. On the other side of the globe is the Antarctic Circle. The area south of this includes the South Pole and is known as the Antarctic.

Latitude lines

Longitude lines

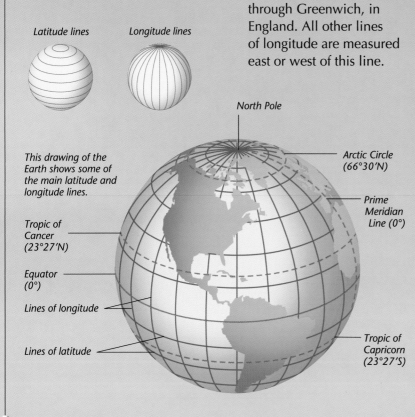

This drawing of the Earth shows some of the main latitude and longitude lines.

North Pole

Arctic Circle (66°30'N)

Prime Meridian Line (0°)

Tropic of Cancer (23°27'N)

Equator (0°)

Lines of longitude

Lines of latitude

Tropic of Capricorn (23°27'S)

Internet links

For links to websites where you can find out more about latitude and longitude and explore the world in an online game, go to **www.usborne-quicklinks.com**

Using the lines

Lines of latitude and longitude are measured in degrees (°). The positions of places are described according to which lines of latitude and longitude are nearest to them. For example, a place with a location of 50°S and 100°E has a latitude 50 degrees south of the Equator, and a longitude 100 degrees east of the Prime Meridian Line.

Exact locations

The distance between degrees is divided up to give even more precise measurements. Each degree is divided into 60 minutes ('), and each minute is divided into 60 seconds ("). The subdivisions allow us to locate any place on Earth. For example, the city of New York, U.S.A., is at 40°42'51"N and 74°00'23"W.

The steamy rainforests of Malaysia lie near the Equator. Many apes, like the one shown here, live in these rainforests.

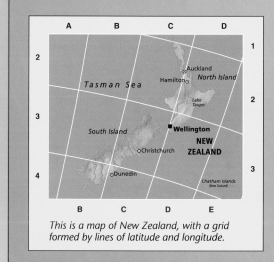

This is a map of New Zealand, with a grid formed by lines of latitude and longitude.

Using a grid

Lines of latitude and longitude form grids on maps. The maps in this book look similar to the one on the left. The columns that run from top to bottom are formed by lines of longitude and marked with letters. The rows running across the page are formed by lines of latitude and are numbered.

All the places listed in the map index on page 130 have a letter and a number reference that tell you where to find them on a particular page. For example, on the map on the left, the city of Christchurch would have a grid reference of C3.

HOW MAPS ARE MADE

The process of making maps is called cartography. Map-makers, or cartographers, compile each map by gathering information about the area and representing it as an image as accurately as possible.

Internet links

For links to websites where you can watch movies of maps made from satellite images and find out how to make a globe from a flat piece of paper, go to
www.usborne-quicklinks.com

Creating maps

Many sources are used to create maps. These include satellite images and aerial photographs. Cartographers often visit the area to be mapped, where they take many extra measurements.

In addition, cartographers use statistics, such as population figures, from censuses and other documents. As the maps are being made, many people check them to make sure they are accurate and up-to-date.

Map projections

Cartographers can't draw maps that show the world exactly as it is, because it is impossible to show a curved surface on a flat map without distorting (stretching or squashing) some areas. A representation of the Earth on a map is called a projection. Projections are worked out using complex mathematics.

There are three basic types of projections – cylindrical, conical and azimuthal, but there are also variations on these. They all distort the Earth's surface in some way, either by altering the shapes or sizes of areas of land or the distance between places.

A cartographer uses an electronic distance measurer to check the measurements of an area of land.

Cylindrical projections

A cylindrical projection is similar to the image created by wrapping a piece of paper around a globe to form a cylinder and then shining a light inside the globe. The shapes of countries would be projected onto the paper. Near the middle they would be accurate, but farther away they would be distorted.

Cartographers often alter the basic cylindrical projection to make the distortion less obvious in certain areas, but they can never make a map that is completely accurate.

This picture of a piece of paper wrapped around a globe illustrates how a cylindrical projection is made.

Below is a type of cylindrical projection called the Mercator projection, which was invented in 1596 by a cartographer named Gerardus Mercator. It makes countries the right shape, but makes those near the poles too big.

This cylindrical projection makes countries the right size in relation to each other, but some parts are too long. The projection was created in 1973 by Arno Peters. It is called the Peters Projection.

Conical projections

A conical projection is similar to the image you would get if you wrapped a cone of paper around part of a globe, then shone a light inside the globe. Where the cone touches the globe, the projection will be most accurate.

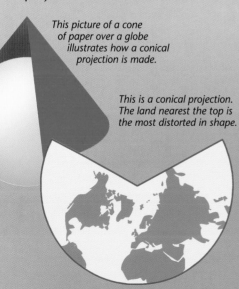

This picture of a cone of paper over a globe illustrates how a conical projection is made.

This is a conical projection. The land nearest the top is the most distorted in shape.

Azimuthal projections

An azimuthal projection is like an image made by holding paper in front of a globe, and shining a light through it. Land projected onto the middle of the paper would be accurate, but areas farther away would be distorted.

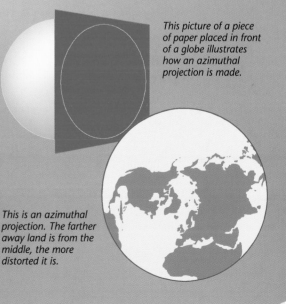

This picture of a piece of paper placed in front of a globe illustrates how an azimuthal projection is made.

This is an azimuthal projection. The farther away land is from the middle, the more distorted it is.

THEMATIC MAPS

Maps that represent information on particular themes, like the ones on these pages, are known as thematic maps. They help you to identify patterns and make comparisons between the features of different areas.

Earth's resources

The Earth contains all kinds of useful resources. Rocks and minerals can be used as building materials, and fuels such as coal, oil and gas contain energy that can be turned into heat and electricity.

Countries with large amounts of natural resources can become very rich. For example, Saudi Arabia, in western Asia, has large oil and gas reserves, which it exports all over the world.

This is an oil field, where oil is extracted from the ground using pumps. It is then piped to refineries and turned into products such as motor fuel.

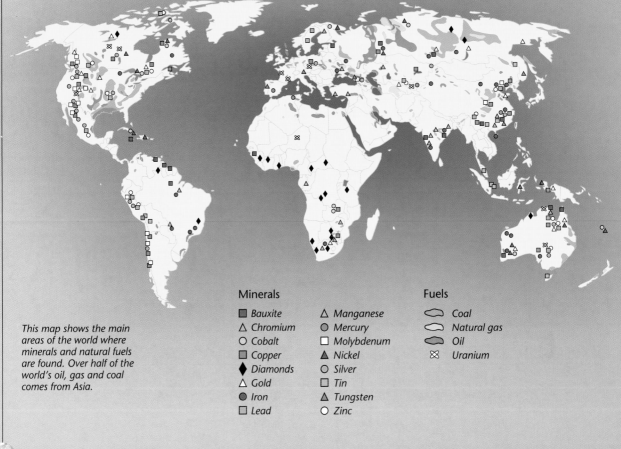

This map shows the main areas of the world where minerals and natural fuels are found. Over half of the world's oil, gas and coal comes from Asia.

Minerals

■ Bauxite	△ Manganese
△ Chromium	◉ Mercury
○ Cobalt	▢ Molybdenum
▢ Copper	▲ Nickel
◆ Diamonds	○ Silver
△ Gold	▢ Tin
● Iron	△ Tungsten
▢ Lead	○ Zinc

Fuels

◠ Coal
◠ Natural gas
◠ Oil
⊠ Uranium

Different climates

The long-term or typical pattern of weather in a particular area is known as its climate. Climates vary across the world and depend largely on each area's latitude. The hottest parts of the world are those closest to the Equator.

Climate is also affected by other factors, such as wind and the height of the land. Oceans influence climate too – places near the sea normally have a milder, wetter climate than areas farther inland.

On this map, land is divided into five climate types. Dry areas are generally hot, but temperatures there can fall very low too. Some dry places, such as the Gobi Desert in eastern Asia, are extremely cold in winter.

☐ Polar
☐ Cold
☐ Temperate
☐ Dry
■ Tropical

World population

There are more than six billion people in the world, and the population is still growing. Experts think it may reach more than nine billion by 2050. The number of people living in a given area is known as its population density. Europe and Asia are the most densely populated continents in the world. About a third of the world's population lives in China and India alone.

Internet links

For a link to a website where you can see the population of the Earth when you were born, and find lots of other population facts, graphs and animations, go to **www.usborne-quicklinks.com**

This map shows the average population density by country. The shading indicates the number of people per sq km (0.386 sq miles).

■ Over 500 people
■ 200–500 people
☐ 100–200 people
☐ 50–100 people
☐ 10–50 people
☐ Fewer than 10 people

HOW TO USE THE MAPS

ach continent section in this atlas begins
with a political map showing the whole
continent. The rest of the maps are larger
scale maps showing the various parts of the
continent in more detail.

Political maps

The shading on the political
maps in this atlas is there to
help you see clearly the
different countries that make
up each continent. The main
purpose of these maps is to
show country borders and
capital cities. Alongside
them there are facts and
figures about the continents
and their features.

*This is a section of the political map of
South America. You can see the whole
map on pages 36–37.*

Environmental maps

The majority of the maps in
this atlas are environmental
maps, like the one on the right.
The shading on these maps
shows different types of land,
or environments, such as
desert, mountain or wetland.

The main key on the opposite
page shows what the different
shading means. It also shows
the symbols used to represent
towns, cities and other
features. There is a smaller key
on each environmental map
repeating the most important
information from this key.

Finding places

To find a particular place or
feature on the environmental
maps, look up its name in
the index on pages 130–143.
Its page number and grid
reference is given next to the
name. You can find out how
to use the grid on page 9.

*The map on the right is part of the
environmental map of the U.S.A. The
numbered labels at the top explain some
important features of these maps.*

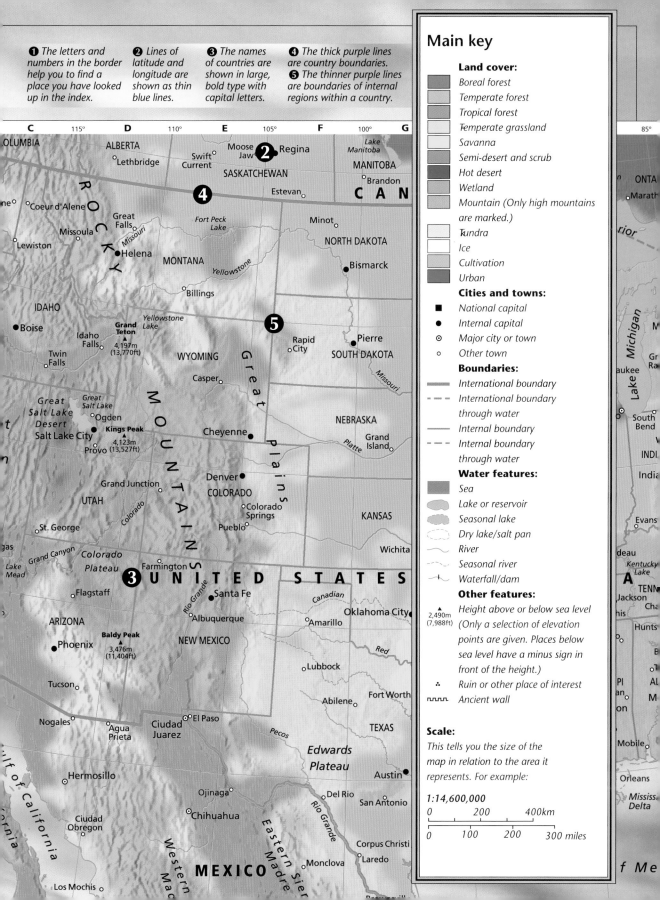

❶ The letters and numbers in the border help you to find a place you have looked up in the index.

❷ Lines of latitude and longitude are shown as thin blue lines.

❸ The names of countries are shown in large, bold type with capital letters.

❹ The thick purple lines are country boundaries.

❺ The thinner purple lines are boundaries of internal regions within a country.

Main key

Land cover:
- Boreal forest
- Temperate forest
- Tropical forest
- Temperate grassland
- Savanna
- Semi-desert and scrub
- Hot desert
- Wetland
- Mountain (Only high mountains are marked.)
- Tundra
- Ice
- Cultivation
- Urban

Cities and towns:
- ■ National capital
- ● Internal capital
- ⊙ Major city or town
- ○ Other town

Boundaries:
- International boundary
- International boundary through water
- Internal boundary
- Internal boundary through water

Water features:
- Sea
- Lake or reservoir
- Seasonal lake
- Dry lake/salt pan
- River
- Seasonal river
- Waterfall/dam

Other features:
- ▲ 2,490m (7,988ft) Height above or below sea level (Only a selection of elevation points are given. Places below sea level have a minus sign in front of the height.)
- ⁂ Ruin or other place of interest
- ⌐⌐⌐ Ancient wall

Scale:
This tells you the size of the map in relation to the area it represents. For example:

1:14,600,000

0   200   400km

0   100   200   300 miles

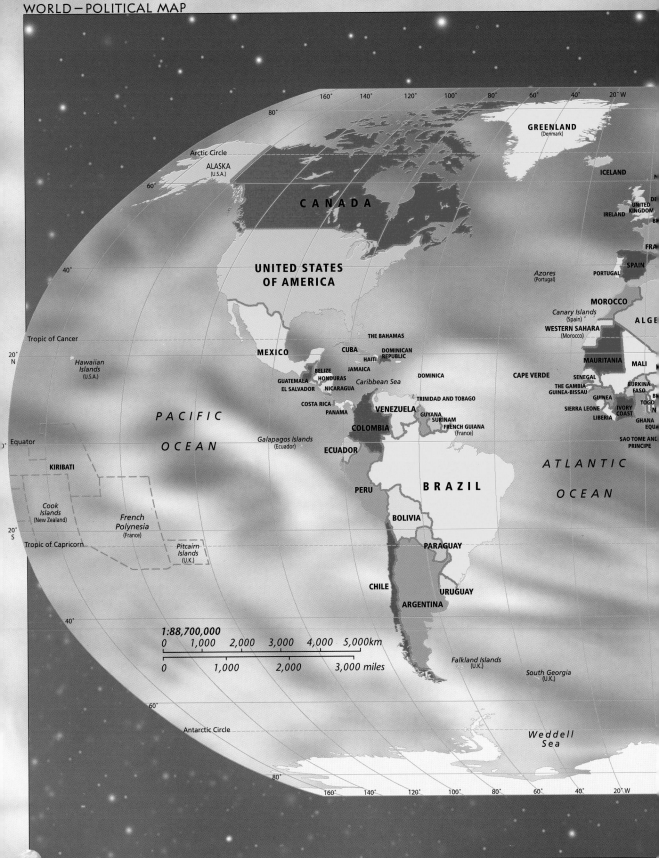

GREENLAND
(Denmark)

ICELAND

Arctic Circle

ALASKA
(U.S.A.)

UNITED
KINGDOM

IRELAND

CANADA

DE

FRA

SPAIN

UNITED STATES
OF AMERICA

Azores
(Portugal)

PORTUGAL

MOROCCO

ALGE

Canary Islands
(Spain)

Tropic of Cancer

WESTERN SAHARA
(Morocco)

20°
N

Hawaiian
Islands
(U.S.A.)

THE BAHAMAS

MEXICO

CUBA

DOMINICAN
REPUBLIC

MAURITANIA

MALI

HAITI

CAPE VERDE

SENEGAL

BELIZE

JAMAICA

DOMINICA

GUATEMALA

HONDURAS

Caribbean Sea

THE GAMBIA
GUINEA-BISSAU

BURKINA
FASO

EL SALVADOR

NICARAGUA

GUINEA

BI

PACIFIC

COSTA RICA

TRINIDAD AND TOBAGO

SIERRA LEONE

TOGO
N

IVORY
COAST

PANAMA

VENEZUELA

GUYANA

LIBERIA

GHANA

OCEAN

COLOMBIA

SURINAM

EQUA

FRENCH GUIANA
(France)

SAO TOME AND
PRINCIPE

ATLANTIC

Galapagos Islands
(Ecuador)

ECUADOR

KIRIBATI

OCEAN

Equator

PERU

BRAZIL

Cook
Islands
(New Zealand)

French
Polynesia
(France)

BOLIVIA

20°
S

Tropic of Capricorn

Pitcairn
Islands
(U.K.)

PARAGUAY

CHILE

URUGUAY

ARGENTINA

40°

1:88,700,000

0   1,000   2,000   3,000   4,000   5,000km

0   1,000   2,000   3,000 miles

Falkland Islands
(U.K.)

South Georgia
(U.K.)

60°

Antarctic Circle

*Weddell
Sea*

80°

40°   60°   80°   100°   120°   140°   160°   180°   80°

Arctic Circle

60°

Svalbard
(Norway)

FINLAND

ESTONIA
LATVIA
RUSSIA   LITHUANIA
POLAND   BELARUS

RUSSIA

CZECH REP.
SLOVAKIA   UKRAINE
HUNGARY   MOLDOVA

ROMANIA
S.M.   BULGARIA   Black Sea
NIA   MAC.   Caspian   KAZAKHSTAN
GREECE   TURKEY   GEORGIA   Sea
ARM.   AZER.   UZBEKISTAN   KYRGYZSTAN

MONGOLIA

40°

Mediterranean Sea   CYPRUS   SYRIA   TURKMENISTAN   TAJIKISTAN
ISRAEL   LEB.   IRAQ   IRAN   AFGHANISTAN   CHINA

JORDAN   KUWAIT   PAKISTAN   NEPAL
LIBYA   EGYPT   BAHRAIN   BHUTAN
SAUDI   QATAR   BANGLA-
ARABIA   U.A.E.   DESH   BURMA

NORTH
KOREA
SOUTH
KOREA

JAPAN

PACIFIC

OCEAN

Tropic of Cancer

20°
N

OMAN   INDIA   (MYANMAR)   TAIWAN
CHAD   ERITREA   YEMEN   LAOS
SUDAN   DJIBOUTI   THAILAND   VIETNAM
CENTRAL   ETHIOPIA   CAMBODIA
AFRICAN   PHILIPPINES
REPUBLIC   SOMALIA   SRI LANKA
CON   UGANDA   MALDIVES   BRUNEI
CONGO   RWANDA   KENYA   MALAYSIA   PALAU
(DEMOCRATIC   BURUNDI   SINGAPORE
REPUBLIC)   TANZANIA   SEYCHELLES   INDONESIA
GOLA   ZAMBIA   MALAWI   COMOROS   INDIAN
ZIMBABWE   MADAGASCAR   MAURITIUS   OCEAN
BIA   BOTSWANA   MOZAMBIQUE   Reunion
(France)
SWAZILAND
LESOTHO
SOUTH AFRICA

Northern
Mariana
Islands
(U.S.A.)

MARSHALL
ISLANDS

FEDERATED STATES
OF MICRONESIA

Equator   0°

NAURU   KIRIBATI

PAPUA
NEW GUINEA   SOLOMON
ISLANDS   TUVALU

SAMOA

Coral Sea
Islands
Territory
(Australia)   VANUATU
New   FIJI   TONGA   20°
Caledonia   S
(France)   Tropic of Capricorn

AUSTRALIA

Kerguelen Islands
(France)

40°

NEW
ZEALAND

SOUTHERN OCEAN

60°

Antarctic Circle

ANTARCTICA

The shading on this map is there to help
you see the different countries clearly.

80°

40°   60°   80°   100°   120°   140°   160°   180°

Abbreviations used on map:

ARM.   ARMENIA
AUST.   AUSTRIA
AZER.   AZERBAIJAN
BELG.   BELGIUM
B.H.   BOSNIA AND HERZEGOVINA
CRO.   CROATIA
CZECH REP.   CZECH REPUBLIC
LEB.   LEBANON
LUX.   LUXEMBOURG
MAC.   MACEDONIA
NETH.   NETHERLANDS
SLOV.   SLOVENIA
S.M.   SERBIA AND MONTENEGRO
SWITZ.   SWITZERLAND
U.A.E.   UNITED ARAB EMIRATES

80°

Beaufort
Sea

Victoria
Island

Queen
Elizabeth
Islands

Ellesmere
Island

Baffin
Island

Baffin
Bay

Greenland

Greenland
Sea

Iceland

Arctic Circle

Alaska

Mount McKinley
▲
6,194m
(20,321ft)

Yukon

Hudson
Bay

Labrador
Sea

British
Isles

60°

Gulf of Alaska

Aleutian Islands

**NORTH
AMERICA**

Rocky Mountains

Great Plains

Great
Lakes

Appalachian Mountains

Newfoundland

Azores

40°

Mississippi

Canary
Islands

Atlas Mour

20°
N

Tropic of Cancer

Hawaiian
Islands

Gulf of
Mexico

Cuba

Greater Antilles

West Indies

Lesser
Antilles

Cape Verde
Islands

Caribbean
Sea

0°

Equator

Polynesia

PACIFIC

Galapagos
Islands

Guiana
Highlands

Amazon
Basin

Amazon

Selvas

ATLANTIC

OCEAN

OCEAN

**SOUTH
AMERICA**

20°
S

Tahiti

Tropic of Capricorn

Andes

Atacama Desert

Easter Island

Aconcagua
▲
6,959m
(22,831ft)

Pampas

Patagonia

40°

1:88,700,000

0   1,000   2,000   3,000   4,000   5,000km

0   1,000   2,000   3,000 miles

Falkland Islands

South Georgia

60°

Cape Horn

Antarctic Circle

Antarctic
Peninsula

Weddell
Sea

80°

160°   140°   120°   100°   80°   60°   40°   20° W

RCTIC OCEAN

40°   60°   80°   100°   Severnaya   140°   160°   180°
                            Zemlya
Svalbard   Novaya   New Siberia   80°
            Zemlya   Kara Sea   Laptev Sea   Islands   East Siberian Sea
th Cape   Barents Sea

ndinavia   Verkhoyansk Range   Arctic Circle

rth European Plain   Ob   Yenisey   S i b e r i a   60°
                              Lake   Sea   Kamchatka
EUROPE   Volga   A S I A   Baikal   of   Peninsula
                                        Okhotsk
Danube   Mount   Aral   Altai Mountains   Gobi   Hokkaido
Black Sea   Elbrus   Sea   Desert   Sea
           5,642m   Caspian   Huang He (Yellow)   of   40°
           (18,510ft)   Sea   Yellow   Japan
diterranean Sea   Zagros Mountains   H i   Sea   Honshu
                                  m a   Chang Jiang (Yangtze)   East
                           l a   China   Tropic of Cancer
                        y a   Sea   20°
e   Nile   Red Sea   Ganges   s   Mount Everest   Taiwan   N
                        Deccan   8,850m
FRICA   Arabian   Plateau   (29,035ft)   Philippine   M i c r o n e s i a   PACIFIC
        Peninsula   Arabian   Bay   Islands
a r a   Sea   of   South
        Ethiopian   Bengal   China   OCEAN
        Highlands   Sri Lanka   Sea   Celebes
Lake   Sea
Victoria   Sumatra   Borneo   Equator
Congo   Kilimanjaro   Seychelles   New Guinea   M e l a n e s i a
Basin   5,895m   I N D I A N   Greater Sunda Islands   Mount Wilhelm
        (19,340ft)   Java   Arafura   4,509m   Solomon
        Comoro   OCEAN   Lesser Sunda Islands   Sea   (14,793ft)   Islands
        Islands   20°
Madagascar   Coral   New   Fiji   S
Mauritius   Great Sandy   Sea   Caledonia   Islands
Reunion   Desert   Tropic of Capricorn
Desert   AUSTRALASIA AND OCEANIA
of Good Hope   Great Victoria   Tasman   North
            Desert   Sea   Island   40°
Kerguelen   Tasmania   South
Islands   Island
                            60°

SOUTHERN OCEAN   Antarctic Circle

A N T A R C T I C A   See page 17 for key.

E   40°   60°   80°   100°   120°   140°   160°   180°   80°

NORTH AMERICA

The name "North America" can be used to mean several different things. In this atlas, North America includes Greenland, Canada, the U.S.A., the Caribbean, and the countries of Central America, which run along the narrow strip of land between the U.S.A. and South America. The continent has over 20 countries, including Canada, the second-largest country in the world.

These are columns of rock called hoodoos in Bryce Canyon National Park, U.S.A.

Arctic Circle

ARCTIC OCEAN

Beaufort Sea

Bering Sea

Yukon

ALASKA (U.S.A.)

Anchorage

Victoria Island

CANADA

Vancouver

Columbia

PACIFIC OCEAN

Hawaiian Islands (U.S.A.)

Los Angeles

UNITED STATE

Colorado

Rio Grande

Tropic of Cancer

MEXICO

Mexico Cit

The shading on this map is there to help you see clearly the different countries that make up the continent.

GREENLAND
(Denmark)

esmere
nd

een
abeth
nds

Baffin
Island

Godthab

Hudson
Bay

Newfoundland

St. Lawrence

Montreal
Ottawa

Great
Lakes

ATLANTIC

OCEAN

Chicago

New York

Washington D.C.

F AMERICA

Mississippi

Tropic of Cancer

Houston

THE
BAHAMAS

Gulf of
Mexico

Havana

CUBA

Puerto Rico
(U.S.A.)

Guadeloupe
(France)

HAITI

DOMINICAN
REPUBLIC

DOMINICA
Martinique (France)

BARBADOS

JAMAICA

TRINIDAD
AND TOBAGO

BELIZE

Caribbean Sea

GUATEMALA

HONDURAS

EL SALVADOR

NICARAGUA

COSTA RICA

PANAMA

Facts

Total land area 22,656,190 sq km (8,745,289 sq miles)
Total population 487 million
Biggest city Mexico City, Mexico
Biggest country Canada 9,970,610 sq km (3,849,653 sq miles)
Smallest country Saint Kitts and Nevis 269 sq km (104 sq miles)

Highest mountain Mount McKinley, Alaska, U.S.A. 6,194m (20,321ft)
Longest river Mississippi/Missouri, U.S.A. 6,019km (3,741 miles)
Biggest lake Lake Superior, between the U.S.A. and Canada 82,414 sq km (31,820 sq miles)
Highest waterfall Yosemite Falls, on the Yosemite Creek, California, U.S.A. 739m (2,425ft)
Biggest desert Great Basin Desert, U.S.A. 492,000 sq km (190,000 sq miles)
Biggest island Greenland 2,175,600 sq km (840,000 sq miles)

Main mineral deposits Silver, gold, copper, lead, zinc, graphite, molybdenum, nickel
Main fuel deposits Oil, coal, natural gas, uranium

The bald eagle is the national bird of the U.S.A. It is not really bald, but has white feathers on its head.

North America covers a huge area, from just south of the North Pole to just north of the Equator. The land in the far north is icy and barren, while southern areas are lush and tropical. The west is dominated by the snow-capped Rocky Mountains.

Enormous parks

North America has many vast national parks. These are specially-protected natural areas where all kinds of animals live. One of the most famous parks is Yellowstone Park in Wyoming, U.S.A., which is home to wolves, black bears and many other animals. The park also has natural hot springs and geysers.

This satellite image of North America shows dry areas in brown, vegetation in green and icy regions in white.

Erupting island

Half of the island of Hawaii is covered by Mauna Loa, the biggest volcano on Earth, and one of the most active. The volcano is monitored constantly to check for impending eruptions. Its biggest eruption was in 1950, when a wide river of red-hot lava flowed 24km (15 miles) to the sea, destroying roads and houses in its path.

This satellite image shows part of Mauna Loa volcano. The dark, round hole at the top is one of the volcano's craters, out of which lava and gases regularly explode.

This huge pool is a natural hot spring in Yellowstone Park, Wyoming, U.S.A. The water heats up under the ground.

Internet links

For links to websites where you can find online tours and maps of the Grand Canyon and Yellowstone Park's hot springs, geysers and wildlife, go to **www.usborne-quicklinks.com**

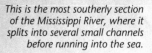

This is the most southerly section of the Mississippi River, where it splits into several small channels before running into the sea.

Mighty Mississippi

The Mississippi/Missouri River is the longest river system in North America and the fourth-longest in the world. The Mississippi flows from Minnesota in northern U.S.A. to the Gulf of Mexico in the south. The Missouri begins in Montana, in the west, and joins the Mississippi in the state of Missouri. The river system is a busy shipping route, and is also vital for wildlife – migratory birds follow it as they fly south in the winter.

The deepest valley

The Grand Canyon, in Arizona, U.S.A., is the world's largest gorge, a deep valley that stretches over 400km (250 miles). In some parts it is 1.6km (1 mile) deep, and up to 29km (18 miles) wide.

The Grand Canyon was carved out by the Colorado River, which eroded the rocky land over many thousands of years. It is possible to hike down the sides of the Canyon, but they are so steep that it takes a whole day to get to the bottom.

Running from top left to bottom right of this satellite image is the jagged Grand Canyon, in the flat, dry state of Arizona, U.S.A. Smaller valleys join the main canyon.

The northern part of North America consists mainly of Canada and the U.S.A. and has many large, dynamic cities as well as forests, deserts and other vast natural spaces.

Huge clouds of spray and mist rise from Horseshoe Falls, one of the two spectacular waterfalls that form Niagara Falls. The falls divide the U.S.A. (left) and Canada (right).

Cold country

Canada has extremely cold, snowy winters, especially in northern and eastern areas. In the city of Montreal, an amazing 1m (40in) of snow once fell in a single day. Not surprisingly, Canada is famous for its many winter sports, such as skiing, ice-skating and ice hockey.

On the border

The border between Canada and the U.S.A. is the longest in the world, covering 6,416km (3,987 miles). In the east, the border runs through several huge lakes, known as the Great Lakes. This section of the border includes Niagara Falls, where water from Lake Erie crashes over two enormous waterfalls.

Big cities

The largest city in the U.S.A. is New York, which is also the country's financial capital. Other big cities include Los Angeles, home of the movie-making area Hollywood, and Las Vegas, which boasts the largest number of hotel rooms of any U.S. city.

At night, the casinos and hotels of Las Vegas are lit up in a blaze of neon lights.

Desert heat

Death Valley in California is the driest place in the U.S.A., and one of the hottest places in the world. The temperature in this vast wilderness has been known to reach a sweltering 57°C (134°F). The desert is generally barren, though when rain does occasionally fall, beautiful wild flowers spring up between the rocks.

An American alligator lazes in one of Florida's coastal swamps. Alligators eat birds, frogs and other animals – sometimes even small alligators.

In the foreground of this Las Vegas skyline is a replica of the Chrysler Building, a New York skyscraper. It is part of an extravagant hotel that has 12 towers, each in the shape of a famous New York building.

The sunshine state

Florida, in southeastern U.S.A., has a hot, tropical climate and is nicknamed "the sunshine state". Southern Florida is covered in swampy wetlands called the Everglades. All kinds of wildlife live there, including Florida panthers and American alligators.

Internet links

For links to websites where you can watch slide shows of U.S. cities, discover more about Canada with a map game and try a test-yourself quiz on Everglades animals, go to **www.usborne-quicklinks.com**

Central America is dominated by the country of Mexico, with its ancient ruins and crowded cities. Farther south, the countries near the border with South America have beautiful beaches, tropical rainforests and fiery volcanoes.

Here a bright wall mural is being painted in the coastal town of Cancun, one of Mexico's lively tourist spots.

City living

Mexico has a huge population, and also has millions of visitors every year. Its biggest city is the capital, Mexico City, where almost a quarter of Mexico's total population lives. The city is so overcrowded that the air is heavily polluted, and many people have poor living conditions and inadequate water supplies.

These statues are in Tula, Mexico. They were built by the ancient Toltec people, and were probably columns that held up a roof.

Ancient remains

In Mexico and nearby areas there are many remains of ancient cities. These were built by people from ancient civilizations, such as the Maya and the Toltec. The Maya had a powerful empire around AD200–900, while the Toltec ruled from about 900 to 1200. These peoples were excellent builders, and created many impressive temples and elaborately carved statues.

Land of volcanoes

Along the Pacific coast of Central America are more than 40 volcanoes. Lava from volcanic eruptions helps make the soil fertile, which is good for growing crops such as bananas and coffee. The volcanoes erupt regularly, and can be very dangerous. For example, the Arenal volcano in Costa Rica wiped out a whole town in a 1963 eruption, and has produced frequent lava flows ever since.

A white-nosed coati raids a banana tree in Costa Rica. These Central American mammals eat all kinds of fruit.

This is the Arenal volcano during a recent eruption. Lava can flow more than 2km (1.5 miles) from the volcano's base.

Sun and storms

The Caribbean islands have stunning sandy beaches and a hot climate. But their position in the Atlantic Ocean means that they are often hit by tropical storms and hurricanes. Some hurricanes reach wind speeds of 250kph (155mph).

Internet links

For links to websites where you can take virtual tours of Mexico and the Caribbean, and discover ancient Mayan sites on an interactive map, go to
www.usborne-quicklinks.com

Linking oceans

The Panama Canal is one of the world's busiest shipping routes. It cuts through the country of Panama and is a short cut for ships sailing between the Atlantic and Pacific oceans. Before the canal opened, ships had to sail around South America, an extra 12,500km (7,800 miles).

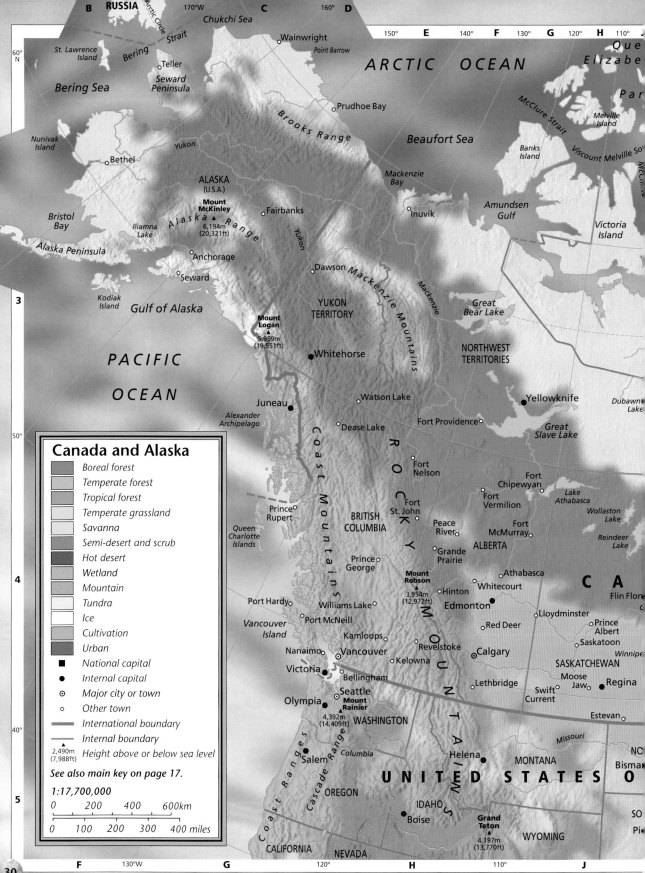

Canada and Alaska

Boreal forest
Temperate forest
Tropical forest
Temperate grassland
Savanna
Semi-desert and scrub
Hot desert
Wetland
Mountain
Tundra
Ice
Cultivation
Urban
■ National capital
● Internal capital
⊙ Major city or town
○ Other town
── International boundary
── Internal boundary
▲ 2,490m (7,988ft) Height above or below sea level

See also main key on page 17.

1:17,700,000

0   200   400   600km
0 100 200 300 400 miles

RUSSIA

Chukchi Sea

ARCTIC OCEAN

Wainwright
Point Barrow

St. Lawrence Island

Teller

Seward Peninsula

Bering Sea

Prudhoe Bay

Brooks Range

Beaufort Sea

Nunivak Island

Bethel

Yukon

ALASKA (U.S.A.)

Mackenzie Bay

Banks Island

McClure Strait

Melville Island

Viscount Melville So

Que Elizabe

Par

Inuvik

Amundsen Gulf

Victoria Island

Bristol Bay

Iliamna Lake

Mount McKinley 6,194m (20,321ft)

Alaska Range

Fairbanks

Alaska Peninsula

Anchorage

Seward

Yukon

Dawson

Mackenzie Mountains

Mackenzie

Great Bear Lake

Kodiak Island

Gulf of Alaska

YUKON TERRITORY

NORTHWEST TERRITORIES

Yellowknife

Dubawn Lake

PACIFIC

OCEAN

Mount Logan 5,959m (19,551ft)

Whitehorse

Juneau

Watson Lake

Fort Providence

Great Slave Lake

Alexander Archipelago

Dease Lake

Prince Rupert

Queen Charlotte Islands

BRITISH COLUMBIA

Fort Nelson

Fort St. John

Coast Mountains

Fort Chipewyan

Fort Vermilion

Fort McMurray

Lake Athabasca

Wollaston Lake

Reindeer Lake

Peace River

Grande Prairie

ALBERTA

Athabasca

Whitecourt

C A

Flin Flon

Port Hardy

Williams Lake

Prince George

Mount Robson 3,954m (12,972ft)

Hinton

Edmonton

Lloydminster

Prince Albert

Saskatoon

Winnipe

Vancouver Island

Port McNeill

Kamloops

Red Deer

SASKATCHEWAN

Nanaimo

Vancouver

Revelstoke

Kelowna

Calgary

Moose Jaw

Regina

Victoria

Bellingham

Lethbridge

Swift Current

Estevan

Seattle

Olympia

Mount Rainier 4,392m (14,409ft)

WASHINGTON

Helena

MONTANA

NO

Bisma

Pi

Salem

Columbia

Cascade Range

Coast Ranges

OREGON

IDAHO

Boise

UNITED STATES O

Grand Teton 4,197m (13,770ft)

WYOMING

SO

CALIFORNIA

NEVADA

30

ROCKY MOUNTAINS

Missouri

lands
Ellesmere
Island

Baffin

Bay

1

A 180° B 170°W C 160°

Bering Sea

55°N 55°N

A l e u t i a n   I s l a n d s

Shishaldin
Volcano

2,857m
(9,372ft) Unimak
Island

3 Attu
Island

Near
Islands

Fox Islands

Unalaska
Island

Umnak
Island

3

ands

st

Devon Island

Lancaster Sound

Somerset
Island

Baffin
Bay

Baffin
Island

2

Rat
Islands

Andreanof Islands

Atka
Island

Umnak
Island

A 180° B 170°W C

Same scale as main map

Boothia
eninsula

Gulf of Boothia

am
nd

Melville
Peninsula

Foxe
Basin

Nettilling
Lake

Cumberland
Peninsula

Davis Strait

GREENLAND
(Denmark)

Cape Farewell

2

3

NUNAVUT

Southampton
Island

Foxe
Peninsula

Amadjuak
Lake

Iqaluit

Labrador Sea

ATLANTIC

Hudson Strait

Cape Chidley

OCEAN

Ivujivik

Ungava
Peninsula

Ungava
Bay

Nain

Makkovik

Cartwright

50°

All islands within Hudson Bay,
James Bay and Ungava Bay lie
within Nunavut.

Kuujjuaq

Inukjuak

NEWFOUNDLAND

Happy Valley-
Goose Bay

Churchill

Hudson Bay

Belcher
Islands

Smallwood
Reservoir

Churchill Falls

Gander

St. John's

ITOBA

Thompson

Fort Severn

La Grande
Reservoir

Labrador
City

QUEBEC

Manicouagan
Reservoir

Anticosti
Island

Newfoundland

Corner Brook

St. Pierre
and Miquelon
(France)

D A

Lake
Winnipeg
nd
ids

James
Bay

Radisson

Fort Albany

Waskaganish

Gulf of
St. Lawrence

Gaspé

Sydney

4

ONTARIO

Lake
Mistassini

Baie-
Comeau

PRINCE
EDWARD
ISLAND

Charlottetown

itoba

Lake
Nipigon

Kirkland Lake

Chicoutimi

Edmundston

Bathurst

NEW
BRUNSWICK

Moncton

Halifax

nipeg
don

Lake
of the
Woods

Dryden

Kenora

Marathon

Thunder Bay

Val-d'Or

Trois-Rivieres

Quebec

Fredericton

Saint
John

NOVA
SCOTIA

Yarmouth

40°

OTA

MINNESOTA

Lake Superior

Sudbury

Sault
Ste. Marie

North Bay

Huntsville

Kingston

Montreal

St. Lawrence

Ottawa

Montpelier

MAINE

Augusta

Concord

MERICA

Lake Huron

MICHIGAN

Owen
Sound

Lake
Ontario

Toronto

Hamilton

London

Niagara
Falls

Buffalo

NEW YORK

Albany

VERMONT

NEW HAMPSHIRE

Boston

MASSACHUSETTS

Providence

RHODE ISLAND

Hartford

5

OTA

Minneapolis

St. Paul

Mississippi

WISCONSIN

Madison

Lake Michigan

Lansing

Detroit

Windsor

Lake Erie

Erie

PENNSYLVANIA

Harrisburg

CONNECTICUT

New York

Trenton

NEW JERSEY

Philadelphia

Dover

DELAWARE

70°

K

Chicago

ILLINOIS

INDIANA

90°

OHIO

80°

Cleveland

Pittsburgh

Columbus

Annapolis

Washington D.C.

N

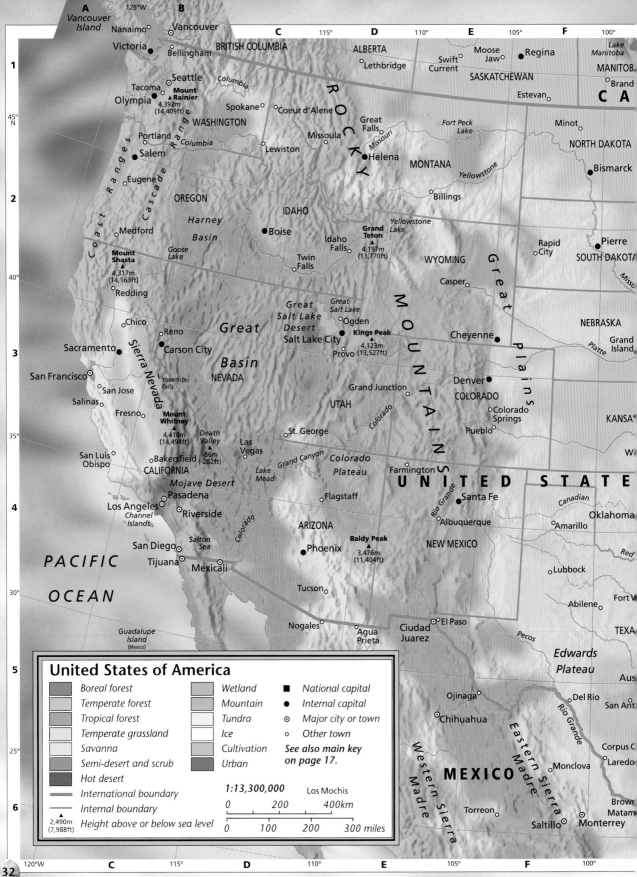

United States of America

Boreal forest	Wetland	■ National capital
Temperate forest	Mountain	● Internal capital
Tropical forest	Tundra	⊙ Major city or town
Temperate grassland	Ice	○ Other town
Savanna	Cultivation	*See also main key on page 17.*
Semi-desert and scrub	Urban	
Hot desert		

International boundary

Internal boundary

▲ 2,490m (7,988ft) Height above or below sea level

1:13,300,000

Los Mochis

0   200   400km

0   100   200   300 miles

Map labels

Vancouver Island
Nanaimo
Victoria
Bellingham
Vancouver
BRITISH COLUMBIA
ALBERTA
Lethbridge
Swift Current
Moose Jaw
Regina
SASKATCHEWAN
Estevan
Lake Manitoba
MANITOBA
Brand
CA

Tacoma
Seattle
Mount Rainier 4,392m (14,409ft)
Olympia
Columbia
Spokane
Coeur d'Alene
Great Falls
Fort Peck Lake
Minot
NORTH DAKOTA
Bismarck

WASHINGTON
Portland
Salem
Columbia
Lewiston
Missoula
Missouri
Helena
MONTANA
Yellowstone
Billings

Eugene
OREGON
Medford
Harney Basin
IDAHO
Boise
Idaho Falls
Grand Teton 4,197m (13,770ft)
Yellowstone Lake
WYOMING
Rapid City
Pierre
SOUTH DAKOTA
Misso

Mount Shasta 4,317m (14,163ft)
Redding
Goose Lake
Twin Falls
Casper
Great Plains
NEBRASKA

Chico
Reno
Carson City
Great Basin
Great Salt Lake Desert
Great Salt Lake
Ogden
Kings Peak 4,123m (13,527ft)
Salt Lake City
Provo
Cheyenne
ROCKY MOUNTAINS
Grand Island

Sacramento
Sierra Nevada
NEVADA
UTAH
Grand Junction
Denver
COLORADO
Platte
Colorado Springs
KANSAS

San Francisco
San Jose
Salinas
Fresno
Yosemite Falls
Mount Whitney 4,418m (14,494ft)
Death Valley -86m (-282ft)
St. George
Las Vegas
Colorado
Colorado Plateau
Pueblo
Wi

San Luis Obispo
Bakersfield
CALIFORNIA
Lake Mead
Grand Canyon
Farmington
Santa Fe
Canadian
Oklahoma

Mojave Desert
Pasadena
Los Angeles
Channel Islands
Riverside
Flagstaff
Rio Grande
Albuquerque
UNITED STATE
Amarillo

San Diego
Tijuana
Salton Sea
Mexicali
ARIZONA
Phoenix
Baldy Peak 3,476m (11,404ft)
NEW MEXICO
Lubbock
Red

PACIFIC OCEAN
Tucson
Nogales
Agua Prieta
Ciudad Juarez
El Paso
Pecos
Abilene
Fort W
TEXA

Guadalupe Island (Mexico)
Ojinaga
Chihuahua
Rio Grande
Edwards Plateau
Aus

Western Sierra Madre
Eastern Sierra Madre
MEXICO
Del Rio
San Ant
Corpus C
Monclova
Laredo

Torreon
Saltillo
Monterrey
Brow
Matam

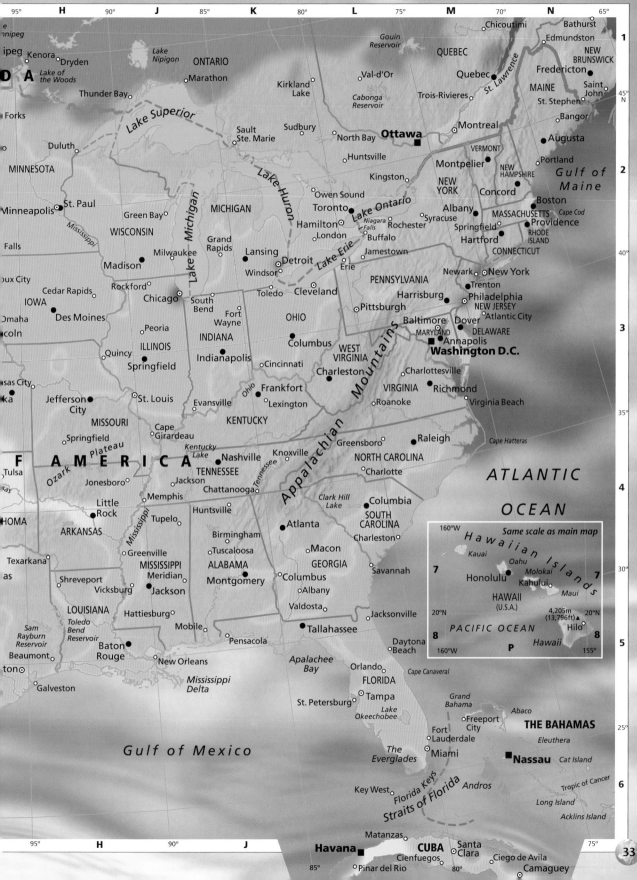

ipeg
Kenora   Dryden
Forks
DA   Lake of
the Woods   Thunder Bay
Duluth   Lake Superior
MINNESOTA
Minneapolis   St. Paul
Falls   Mississippi
ux City   Green Bay   WISCONSIN
Cedar Rapids   Madison   Milwaukee
IOWA   Rockford
Omaha   Des Moines   Chicago
coln   ILLINOIS   Peoria
sas City   Quincy   Springfield
ka   Jefferson   St. Louis
City   MISSOURI
Springfield   Cape
Girardeau
Tulsa   Ozark   Plateau   Kentucky
AMERICA   Lake
OMA   Jonesboro   Jackson   Nashville
as   Little   Memphis   Huntsville
Rock   ARKANSAS   Tupelo
Texarkana   Greenville   MISSISSIPPI
as   Shreveport   Meridian   Montgomery
Vicksburg   Jackson
LOUISIANA   Hattiesburg   ALABAMA
Sam   Toledo
Rayburn   Bend
Reservoir   Reservoir   Baton   Mobile
Beaumont   Rouge   Pensacola
ton   New Orleans
Galveston   Mississippi
Delta

Lake
Nipigon
ONTARIO
Marathon

Kirkland
Lake
Sault
Ste. Marie   Sudbury
Huntsville
Lake Michigan   MICHIGAN
Owen Sound
Lake Huron   Toronto
Grand   Hamilton
Rapids   Lansing   London
Detroit   Lake Erie   Buffalo
Windsor   Erie
South   Toledo   Cleveland
Bend   Fort
Wayne   OHIO
INDIANA   Columbus
Indianapolis   Cincinnati
Ohio   Frankfort
Evansville   Lexington
KENTUCKY   WEST
VIRGINIA
TENNESSEE   Knoxville   Greensboro
Chattanooga   Charlotte
NORTH CAROLINA
Tennessee   Appalachian   Mountains
Birmingham   Clark Hill   Columbia
Tuscaloosa   Lake   SOUTH
Macon   CAROLINA
GEORGIA   Charleston
Columbus   Savannah
Albany
Valdosta   Jacksonville

Gouin
Reservoir
QUEBEC
Val-d'Or
Cabonga   Quebec
Reservoir   Trois-Rivieres
Ottawa   St. Lawrence
North Bay   Montreal   MAINE
St. Stephen
Montpelier   VERMONT   Portland
Kingston   NEW   NEW
YORK   HAMPSHIRE   Gulf of
Lake Ontario   Concord   Maine
Niagara   Albany   Syracuse   Boston   Cape Cod
Falls   Rochester   Springfield   MASSACHUSETTS   Providence
Hartford   RHODE
Jamestown   CONNECTICUT   ISLAND
Newark   New York
PENNSYLVANIA   Trenton
Harrisburg   Philadelphia
Pittsburgh   NEW JERSEY   Atlantic City
Baltimore   Dover
MARYLAND   Annapolis   DELAWARE
Charleston   Washington D.C.
Charlottesville
VIRGINIA   Richmond
Roanoke   Virginia Beach
Cape Hatteras
Raleigh

Chicoutimi   Bathurst
Edmundston
NEW
BRUNSWICK
Fredericton
Saint
St. Stephen   John
Bangor
Augusta
Portland

ATLANTIC
OCEAN

THE BAHAMAS
Nassau

Florida
St. Petersburg   Tampa
Lake
Okeechobee
Orlando   Cape Canaveral
Daytona
Beach

Gulf of Mexico

Key West   Florida Keys   Andros
Straits of Florida
Matanzas
Havana   CUBA   Santa
Clara
Cienfuegos   Ciego de Avila
Pinar del Rio   Camaguey

Grand
Bahama   Abaco
Freeport
City   Eleuthera
Fort
Lauderdale   Cat Island
Miami
The
Everglades   Long Island
Tropic of Cancer   Acklins Island

Apalachee
Bay

160°W	Same scale as main map
Hawaiian Islands	

Kauai
Oahu
Honolulu   Molokai
Kahului
HAWAII   Maui
(U.S.A.)
20°N   4,205m
(13,796ft)▲   20°N
PACIFIC OCEAN   Hilo
Hawaii
160°W   155°W

120°W   **A**   115°   **B**   110°   **C**   105°   **D**   100°   **E**   95°   **F**   90°

1

CALIFORNIA
San Diego
Tijuana
Mexicali
Phoenix
ARIZONA
NEW MEXICO
Tucson
El Paso
Ciudad Juarez
UNITED STATES OF AMERICA
OKLAHOMA
Lubbock
ARKANSAS
Little Rock
Fort Worth
Dallas
Texarkana
Shreveport
Jackson
Tupel
MISSISSIPPI

30°N
Nogales
Agua Prieta
Abilene
TEXAS
Waco
LOUISIANA
Hattiesburg
Red
Mississippi

2

Guadalupe Island (Mexico)
Cedros Island
Point Eugenia
Hermosillo
Ciudad Obregon
Ojinaga
Chihuahua
Edwards Plateau
Austin
San Antonio
Houston
Galveston
Baton Rouge
New Orle
Missis De
Pecos
Rio Grande

25°
Tropic of Cancer
La Paz
Los Mochis
Culiacan
Durango
Plateau of Mexico
Monclova
Laredo
Corpus Christi
Brownsville
Matamoros
Monterrey
Saltillo
Torreon

3

Cape San Lucas
Mazatlan
Matehuala
San Luis Potosi
4,054m (13,300ft)
Ciudad Victoria
Gulf of Mexic

20°
Revillagigedo Islands (Mexico)
MEXICO
Aguascalientes
Tampico
Merida
Yuca Penin

Puerto Vallarta
Leon
Celaya
Bay of Campeche
Campec

4
Guadalajara
Colima
Morelia
Uruapan
Teotihuacan
Mexico City
Puebla
Orizaba 5,610m (18,405ft)
Veracruz
Tehuacan
Coatzacoalcos
Ciudad del Carm
Villahermosa
Belmop
Tikal

15°
Acapulco
Southern Sierra Madre
Oaxaca
Isthmus of Tehuantepec
Juchitan
Tuxtla Gutierrez
B

Tajumulco 4,220m (13,845ft)
GUATEMAL
Gulf of Tehuantepec
5
Tapachula
Quezaltena
Guatemala City
San Salvador
EL SALV

PACIFIC OCEAN

6

7

Galapagos Islands (Ecuador)

8
Equator
Puerto Ayora

Inset map (1:8,900,000)

65°W   **L**   **M**   60°   **N**

3
Virgin Islands (U.K.)
ATLANTIC OCEAN
San Juan
Puerto Rico (U.S.A.)
Virgin Islands (U.S.A.)
Anguilla (U.K.)
St. Martin (France and Netherlands)
ANTIGUA AND BARBUDA
St. John's
Leeward Islands

4
Basseterre
ST. KITTS AND NEVIS
Montserrat (U.K.)
Guadeloupe (France)
Basse-Terre
Windward Islands

1:8,900,000
0   100   200km
0   50   100 miles
DOMINICA
Roseau
15°N

6
Martinique (France)
Fort-de-France
Caribbean Sea
Castries
ST. LUCIA
5°N
BARBADOS
Kingstown
ST. VINCENT AND THE GRENADINES
Bridgetown

7
Lesser Antilles
St. George's
GRENADA

Margarita Island
Porlamar
Tobago
Port-of-Spain
TRINIDAD AND TOBAGO
Trinidad

8
Cumana
VENEZUELA
65°W   **L**   **M**   60°   **N**
Equator

Central America and the Caribbean

Key

- Boreal forest
- Temperate forest
- Tropical forest
- Temperate grassland
- Savanna
- Semi-desert and scrub
- Hot desert
- International boundary
- Internal boundary
- 2,490m (7,988ft) Height above or below sea level
- Wetland
- Mountain
- Tundra
- Ice
- Cultivation
- Urban
- ■ National capital
- ● Internal capital
- ⊙ Major city or town
- ○ Other town

See also main key on page 17.

1:17,700,000

0   200   400   600km

0   100   200   300   400 miles

ATLANTIC OCEAN

Tropic of Cancer

United States

- ingham
- Atlanta
- Columbia
- NORTH CAROLINA
- GEORGIA
- Macon
- SOUTH CAROLINA
- AMA
- Columbus
- Charleston
- ntgomery
- Savannah
- Albany
- acola
- Tallahassee
- FLORIDA
- Daytona Beach
- Apalachee Bay
- Orlando
- Cape Canaveral
- St. Petersburg
- Tampa
- Lake Okeechobee
- The Everglades
- Miami
- Key West
- Florida Keys
- Straits of Florida

The Bahamas

- Grand Bahama
- Freeport City
- Abaco
- Eleuthera
- Nassau THE BAHAMAS
- Cat Island
- Andros
- Long Island
- Acklins Island
- Great Inagua
- Turks and Caicos Islands (U.K.)

Cuba

- Havana
- Matanzas
- Pinar del Rio
- Santa Clara
- Cienfuegos
- CUBA
- Camaguey
- Holguin
- Isle of Youth
- Bayamo
- Guantanamo
- ancun
- Santiago de Cuba
- Cayman Islands (U.K.)
- Montego Bay
- Swan Islands (Honduras)
- JAMAICA
- Kingston
- Greater Antilles
- Windward Passage
- Cap-Haitien
- Gonaives
- Les Cayes
- HAITI
- Port-au-Prince
- Hispaniola

Dominican Republic

- DOMINICAN REPUBLIC
- Santiago
- La Romana
- Santo Domingo
- San Juan
- Ponce
- Virgin Islands (U.K.)
- Puerto Rico (U.S.A.)
- Leeward Islands
- ANTIGUA AND BARBUDA
- ST. KITTS AND NEVIS
- Guadeloupe (France)
- Windward Islands
- DOMINICA
- Martinique (France)
- ST. LUCIA
- ST. VINCENT AND THE GRENADINES
- BARBADOS
- Lesser Antilles
- GRENADA

Caribbean Sea

Central America

- HONDURAS
- gucigalpa
- Puerto Cabezas
- Matagalpa
- on
- NICARAGUA
- Managua
- Lake Nicaragua
- as
- eriao
- ntarenaso
- Limon
- Gulf of Mosquitos
- STA RICA
- San Jose
- COSTA RICA
- Almirante
- PANAMA
- Colon
- Panama City
- David
- Santiago
- Panama Canal
- La Palma
- Gulf of Panama
- Coiba Island
- San Andres Island (Colombia)

Colombia / Venezuela

- Cape Gallinas
- Aruba (Netherlands)
- Netherlands Antilles (Netherlands)
- Willemstad
- Margarita Island
- Riohacha
- Paraguaipoa
- Gulf of Venezuela
- Santa Marta
- Barranquilla
- Cristobal Colon 5,775m (18,947ft)
- Cartagena
- Cucuta
- Maracaibo
- Lake Maracaibo
- Valera
- Caracas
- Valencia
- Maracay
- Barcelona
- Cumana
- Barquisimeto
- Maturin
- VENEZUELA
- Ciudad Bolivar
- Ciudad Guayana
- Orinoco Delta
- Port-of-Spain
- TRINIDAD AND TOBAGO
- Georgetown
- GUYANA
- Angel Falls
- Mount Roraima 2,810m (9,219ft)
- Santa Elena
- Guiana Highlands
- Boa Vista
- BRAZIL
- Gulf of Darien
- Sincelejo
- Bolivar Peak 5,007m (16,427ft)
- San Fernando de Apure
- San Cristobal
- Pamplona
- Bucaramanga
- Puerto Paez
- Llanos
- Orinoco
- Puerto Inirida
- Colon
- Panama
- Dabeiba
- Medellin
- Quibdo
- Tunja
- Manizales
- Pereira
- Ibague
- Bogota
- COLOMBIA
- Buenaventura
- Western Cordillera
- Cali
- Neiva
- 5,750m (18,865ft) Popayan
- Eastern Cordillera
- Guaviare
- Puerto Inirida
- San Jose del Guaviare
- Tumaco
- Esmeraldas
- Pasto
- Ipiales
- Florencia
- Puerto Leguizamo
- ECUADOR
- Quito
- Ibarra
- Equator
- Negro
- Malpelo Island (Colombia)
- os d ica)

35

Copyright © Usborne Publishing Ltd.

SOUTH AMERICA

South America is made up of 12 independent countries, along with French Guiana, which belongs to France. The continent's biggest and most industrialized country is Brazil, which covers about half of the total land. Brazil is also home to half of South America's population.

This is a guanaco. Guanacos are members of the camel family that live in South America. Guanaco hair is used to make textiles.

Caribbean Sea

Caracas

VENEZUELA

Medellin○ ■Bogota

COLOMBIA Orinoco

Quito■ Equator

ECUADOR Ma

Galapagos
Islands
(Ecuador) Guayaquil○

PERU

Lima■

BOLIVIA

La Paz■ ■Suc

CHILE

PACIFIC

OCEAN Tropic of Capricorn

Santiago■ ○Mendoza

ARGENTI

Cape Horn

Drake Pass

The shading on this map is there to help you see clearly the different countries that make up the continent.

eorgetown
Paramaribo
ANA ■ **Cayenne**
URINAM **FRENCH**
GUIANA
(France)

azon

Equator

○ Recife

B R A Z I L

■ **Brasilia**

○ Belo Horizonte

Parana

RAGUAY Sao Paulo ○ ○ Rio de Janeiro

Asuncion Tropic of Capricorn

○ Porto Alegre

A T L A N T I C

O C E A N

RUGUAY
■ **Montevideo**
■ **enos Aires**

lkland Islands
(U.K.)

This is a red-eyed tree frog. These frogs live in rainforests in South and Central America.

Facts

Total land area 17,866,130 sq km (6,898,113 sq miles)
Total population 346 million
Biggest city Sao Paulo, Brazil
Biggest country Brazil 8,547,400 sq km (3,300,151 sq miles)
Smallest country Surinam 163,270 sq km (63,039 sq miles)

Highest mountain Aconcagua, Argentina 6,959m (22,831ft)
Longest river Amazon, mainly in Brazil 6,440km (4,000 miles)
Biggest lake Lake Maracaibo, Venezuela 13,312 sq km (5,140 sq miles)
Highest waterfall Angel Falls, on the Churun River, Venezuela 979m (3,212ft)
Biggest desert Patagonian Desert, Argentina 673,000 sq km (260,000 sq miles)
Biggest island Tierra del Fuego 46,360 sq km (17,900 sq miles)

Main mineral deposits Copper, tin, molybdenum, bauxite, emeralds
Main fuel deposits Oil, coal

37

South America has a varied and dramatic landscape. In the north there are lush, tropical rainforests, and in central areas are grassy plains, called pampas. In the far south there are glaciers, which are huge, slow-moving masses of ice.

The big picture

The Andes mountain range stretches more than 7,250km (4,500 miles) down the whole length of western South America. It is the longest chain of mountains on Earth.

South America also has the second-longest river in the world, the Amazon. It snakes through the northern half of the continent, from the Andes in Peru to the coast of Brazil, and carries around one-fifth of the world's fresh water.

On this satellite image of South America the Andes mountains are clearly visible in the west. The range contains many active volcanoes.

This flock of large birds, called scarlet ibises, is flying over lush forest in Venezuela.

Icy lands

The southern tip of South America is near Antarctica, which means that the climate is extremely cold. There are glaciers in the mountainous regions, and icebergs in the area's many lakes. South America's most southerly point is Cape Horn. The seas around it are rough and stormy, which can make sailing around Cape Horn very dangerous.

The bluish-white shape in the middle of this image is part of a huge glacier. Melting ice gradually flows into Lake Viedma, shown in the bottom right.

Internet links

For links to websites where you can watch slide shows of Peru's people and places and visit Brazil, Argentina and other South American countries, go to **www.usborne-quicklinks.com**

Water source

On the border of Brazil and Paraguay is a vast expanse of water, about 1,350 sq km (520 sq miles) in size. This is the Itaipu reservoir, a man-made water source which provides water for homes, farms and factories in many areas of Brazil and Paraguay. In the past there had been many droughts, so the reservoir was built to provide a reliable supply of water.

This large blue area is part of the huge Itaipu reservoir, which forms part of the border between Paraguay (left) and Brazil (right).

The river running down the lower part of this image is the Parana River. It flows southward on the eastern side of South America.

This is a mountainous part of the Atacama Desert. In the middle are two snow-capped volcanoes, and on the right are white areas of salt from evaporated salt lakes.

The driest desert

Running down the western coast of Chile is the Atacama Desert, the driest place on Earth. Many areas of the desert go for decades without rain and in some parts rainfall has never been recorded.

Vast areas of the desert are covered in salt, which is all that is left of evaporated saltwater lakes. The rocky landscape looks like the Moon's surface, and NASA vehicles have been tested there in preparation for crossing the Moon's rugged terrain.

One of South America's main features is the Amazon rainforest. This is the largest rainforest in the world, covering an area nearly the size of Europe. The continent also has fascinating cities, both ancient and modern.

Parrot snakes live in trees in the Amazon rainforest. They often open their mouths wide like this to scare off predators.

Machu Picchu

High in the Andes Mountains of Peru lies the ancient, ruined city of Machu Picchu. It was built by the Incas, the South American people who ruled the western part of the continent from about 1400 to 1530. The city contains the ruins of many stone buildings, such as temples, palaces and storerooms, which were built around large central courtyards.

This is Machu Picchu, in the Andes. The city's buildings were constructed on wide steps cut into the sloping ground.

Amazing Amazon

The Amazon rainforest spreads across northern South America and is home to one-third of all the world's animal species. The rainforest contains over 100 species of snakes, from rare boa constrictors to common green parrot snakes.

Here is part of the wealthy, crowded financial district in Santiago, Chile.

City sprawl

South America has many huge cities, such as Sao Paulo in Brazil and Santiago in Chile. The growth of business and industry in these cities has led to the creation of towering skyscrapers, but also causes extra traffic and pollution. The cities are so overcrowded that many people live in poor, run-down suburbs.

Island animals

The Galapagos Islands are a cluster of small, rocky islands that lie in the Pacific Ocean, about 1,000km (600 miles) off the coast of Ecuador.

The islands are home to all kinds of unusual animals, such as giant tortoises. These enormous creatures weigh up to 250kg (550lb), and can live for more than a hundred years. Many tropical birds live on the islands too, including Galapagos penguins and frigate birds.

Fantastic falls

South America's mountainous landscape has led to the formation of many waterfalls, including Angel Falls in Venezuela, which is the world's biggest waterfall. It is 979m (3,212ft) high, more than twice the height of the tallest building in the world.

A male frigate bird puffs out his bright red pouch to attract females. Frigate birds live on many of the Galapagos Islands.

Internet links

For links to websites where you can watch a movie about the Amazon rainforest and take a virtual tour of Machu Picchu, go to **www.usborne-quicklinks.com**

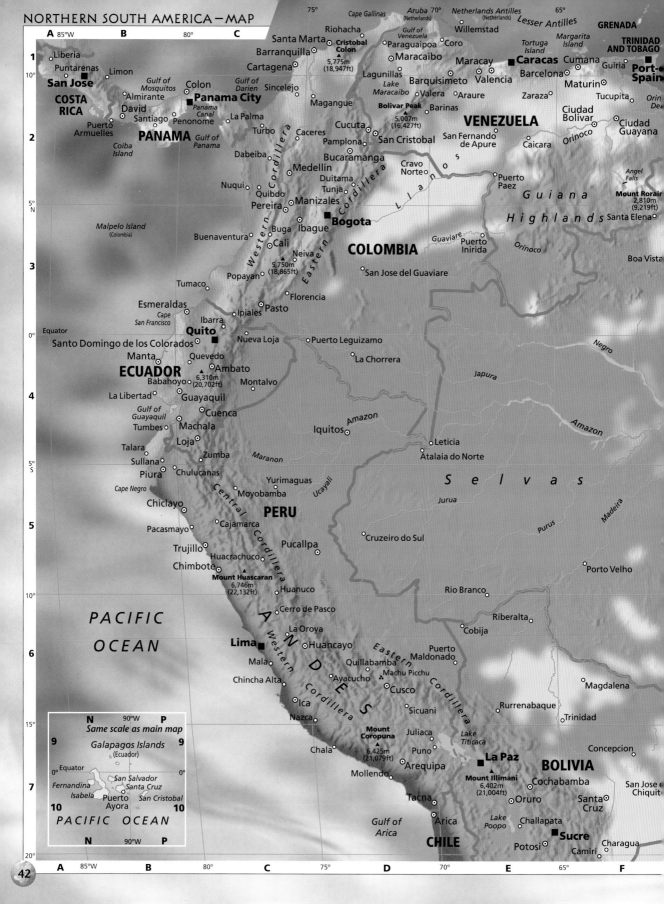

A 85°W   B   80°   C

Liberia
Puntarenas   Limon
San Jose   COSTA   RICA
Gulf of Mosquitos
Colon
Almirante   Panama City
David   Panama Canal
Santiago   Penonome
Puerto Armuelles   La Palma
PANAMA   Gulf of Panama
Coiba Island
Malpelo Island (Colombia)

Cape Gallinas
Aruba 70°   Netherlands Antilles (Netherlands)   65°   GRENADA
(Netherlands)   Lesser Antilles
Santa Marta   Willemstad
Barranquilla   Cristobal Colon 5,775m (18,947ft)   Gulf of Venezuela   Coro   Tortuga Island   Margarita Island   TRINIDAD AND TOBAGO
Cartagena   Paraguaipoa   Maracaibo   Maracay   Caracas   Cumana   Guiria   Port-Spain
Riohacha   Santa Marta   Lagunillas   Barquisimeto   Barcelona   Maturin   Tucupita   Orin De
Sincelejo   Lake Maracaibo   Valera   Araure   Zaraza   Ciudad Bolivar   Ciudad Guayana
Magangue   Bolivar Peak 5,007m (16,427ft)   Barinas   San Fernando de Apure   Caicara   Orinoco
Turbo   Caceres   Cucuta   Pamplona   San Cristobal   VENEZUELA   Puerto Paez   Angel Falls   Mount Rorair 2,810m (9,219ft)
Dabeiba   Bucaramanga   Cravo Norteo   Guiana   Santa Elena
Nuqui   Medellin   Duitama   Tunja   Llanos   Highlands   Boa Vista
Quibdo   Manizales   Puerto Inirida   Orinoco
Pereira   Bogota   Guaviare   Puerto Inirida
Buenaventura   Buga   Ibague   COLOMBIA   San Jose del Guaviare
Cali   Neiva
Popayan   5,750m (18,865ft)   Florencia
Tumaco   Pasto   Puerto Leguizamo
Esmeraldas   Ipiales   La Chorrera
Cape San Francisco   Ibarra   Nueva Loja   Japura   Negro
Quito   Quevedo
Santo Domingo de los Colorados   La Chorrera
Manta   Ambato   Amazon   Leticia
ECUADOR   Babahoyo   6,310m (20,702ft)   Montalvo   Iquitos   Atalaia do Norte   Amazon
La Libertad   Guayaquil   Cuenca   Maranon
Gulf of Guayaquil   Machala   Yurimaguas   Selvas
Tumbes   Loja   Moyobamba   Jurua
Talara   Zumba   PERU   Purus   Madeira
Sullana   Chulucanas   Pucallpa   Porto Velho
Piura   Cajamarca   Cruzeiro do Sul
Cape Negro   Chiclayo   Trujillo   Huacrachuco
Pacasmayo   Mount Huascaran 6,746m (22,132ft)   Huanuco   Rio Branco   Riberalta
Chimbote   Cerro de Pasco   Cobija   Magdalena
PACIFIC   La Oroya   Puerto Maldonado   Rurrenabaque
OCEAN   Lima   Huancayo   Trinidad
Mala   Quillabamba   Machu Picchu
Chincha Alta   Ayacucho   Cusco
Ica   Sicuani   Concepcion
Nazca   Mount Coropuna 6,425m (21,079ft)   Juliaca   Lake Titicaca   La Paz   BOLIVIA
Chala   Puno   Cochabamba   San Jose Chiquit
Mollendo   Arequipa   Mount Illimani 6,402m (21,004ft)   Oruro   Santa Cruz
Tacna   Challapata   Potosi   Sucre   Charagua
Gulf of Arica   Arica   Lake Poopo   Camiri
CHILE   ANDES   Eastern Cordillera   Western Cordillera   Central Cordillera

Same scale as main map
N   90°W   P
9   Galapagos Islands (Ecuador)   9
0°   Equator   0°
Fernandina   San Salvador
Isabela   Santa Cruz
Puerto Ayora   San Cristobal
10   10
PACIFIC OCEAN
N   90°W   P

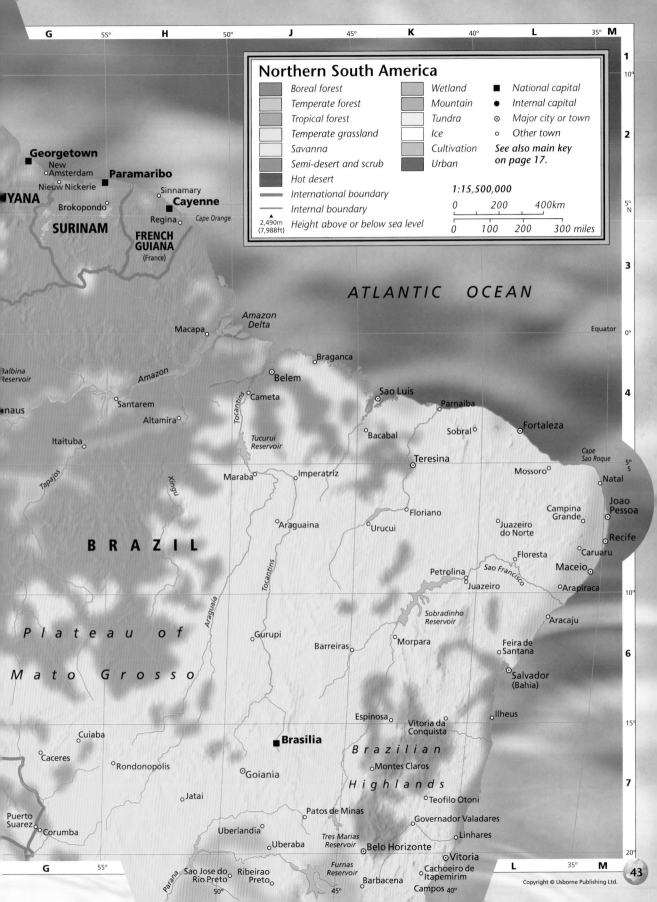

Southern South America

Key

	Boreal forest
	Temperate forest
	Tropical forest
	Temperate grassland
	Savanna
	Semi-desert and scrub
	Hot desert
	Wetland
	Mountain
	Tundra
	Ice
	Cultivation
	Urban
■	National capital
●	Internal capital
⊙	Major city or town
○	Other town
	International boundary
	Internal boundary
▲ 2,490m (7,988ft)	Height above or below sea level

See also main key on page 17.

1:15,500,000

0   100   200   300   400km

0   100   200   300 miles

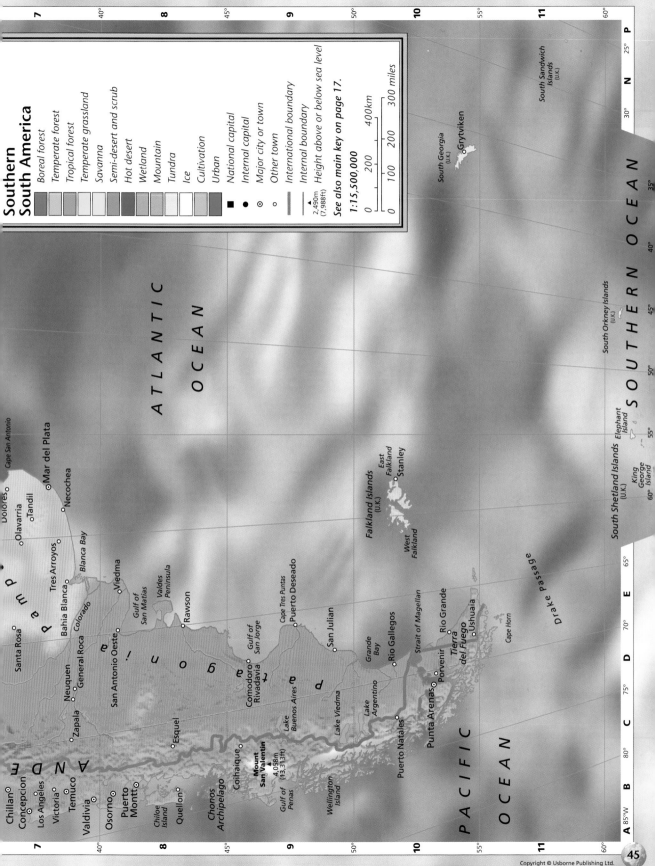

ATLANTIC OCEAN

PACIFIC OCEAN

SOUTHERN OCEAN

Cape San Antonio

Mar del Plata

Dolores
Necochea
Tandil
Olavarria
Tres Arroyos
Blanca Bay
Santa Rosa
Bahia Blanca
Viedma
Colorado
Gulf of San Matias
Valdes Peninsula
Rawson
General Roca
San Antonio Oeste
Neuquen
Zapala

Chillan
Concepcion
Los Angeles
Victoria
Temuco
Valdivia
Osorno
Puerto Montt
Chiloe Island
Quellon
Chonos Archipelago
Esquel

Coihaique
Mount San Valentin
4,058m (13,313ft)
Wellington Island
Gulf of Penas
Puerto Natales
Punta Arenas
Porvenir
Tierra del Fuego
Ushuaia
Cape Horn
Drake Passage

Comodoro Rivadavia
Gulf of San Jorge
Lake Buenos Aires
Lake Viedma
Lake Argentino
Grande Bay
Rio Gallegos
Strait of Magellan
Rio Grande

Cape Tres Puntas
Puerto Deseado
San Julian

Falkland Islands (U.K.)
East Falkland
Stanley
West Falkland

South Georgia (U.K.)
Grytviken

South Sandwich Islands (U.K.)

South Orkney Islands (U.K.)

South Shetland Islands (U.K.)
Elephant Island
King George Island

Pampas
Patagonia
Andes

Copyright © Usborne Publishing Ltd.

45

AUSTRALASIA AND OCEANIA

Australasia is made up of Australia, New Zealand and Papua New Guinea. Oceania is a collection of over 20,000 islands stretching out into the Pacific Ocean.

Northern Mariana Islands
(U.S.A.)

Guam (U.S.A.)

MARSHALL ISLANDS

Koror ▪

Palikir ▪

Majuro ▪

PALAU

FEDERATED STATES
OF MICRONESIA

Bairiki ▪

Equator

Yaren ▪

PAPUA
NEW GUINEA

NAURU

KIRIBAT

INDIAN

New Guinea

SOLOMON
ISLANDS

TUVALU
Funafuti ▪

OCEAN

Arafura
Sea

Port
Moresby ▪

Honiara ▪

SAMO

Coral Sea Islands
Territory
(Australia)

VANUATU

Wallis and
Futuna
(France)

A

FIJI

Coral
Sea

New
Caledonia
(France)

Port-Vila ▪

Suva ▪

TONG

Noumea ○

Nukualofa ▪

Tropic of Capricorn

AUSTRALIA

Brisbane ○

NEW
ZEALAND

Darling

Auckland ○

North Island

Perth ○

Adelaide ○

Sydney ○

Murray

Canberra ▪

Wellington ▪

Melbourne ○

Tasmania

Tasman

Christchurch ○

South Island

Sea

International Date Line

International Date Line

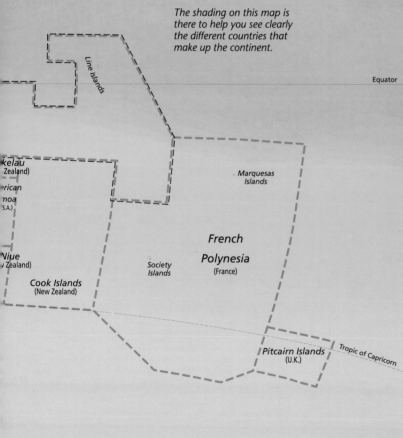

This small island belongs to Papua New Guinea.

PACIFIC OCEAN

The shading on this map is there to help you see clearly the different countries that make up the continent.

Line Islands

Equator

kelau
(Zealand)

rican
noa
S.A.)

Marquesas
Islands

Niue
Zealand)

Society
Islands

French
Polynesia
(France)

Cook Islands
(New Zealand)

Pitcairn Islands
(U.K.)

Tropic of Capricorn

Facts

Total land area 8,564,400 sq km (3,306,715 sq miles)

Total population 31 million

Biggest city Sydney, Australia

Biggest country Australia 7,686,850 sq km (2,967,124 sq miles)

Smallest country Nauru 21 sq km (8 sq miles)

Highest mountain Mount Wilhelm, Papua New Guinea 4,509m (14,793ft)

Longest river Murray/Darling River, Australia 3,718km (2,310 miles)

Biggest lake Lake Eyre, Australia 9,000 sq km (3,470 sq miles)

Highest waterfall Sutherland Falls, on the Arthur River, New Zealand 580m (1,904ft)

Biggest desert Great Victoria Desert, Australia 388,500 sq km (150,000 sq miles)

Biggest island New Guinea 800,000 sq km (309,000 sq miles) (Australia is counted as a continental land mass and not as an island.)

Main mineral deposits Iron, nickel, precious stones, lead, bauxite

Main fuel deposits Oil, coal, uranium

The Moorish idol fish is found in shallow waters throughout the Pacific. It has very bold stripes and a long, distinctive snout.

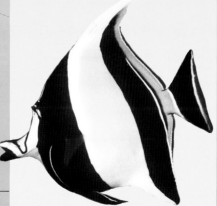

47

Australasia and Oceania's climate is generally very hot. New Zealand and Papua New Guinea are both lush, while Australia is mostly barren. The tiny tropical islands that make up Oceania are surrounded by vast areas of open sea.

This image shows a section of the Southern Alps of South Island, New Zealand. The two turquoise patches are Lake Pukaki and Lake Tekapo.

In this satellite view of Australasia and Oceania, areas of vegetation are green and desert areas are yellow.

Milky waters

New Zealand has two main islands, North Island and South Island, and several smaller ones. On South Island there is a mountain range called the Southern Alps, which has some dramatic milky-turquoise lakes. Their cloudy appearance is caused by rock dust, which is collected, finely ground and then deposited in the lake by glaciers. The rock dust is so fine, it stays suspended in the water, instead of sinking.

Land of bushfires

Most of Australia is hot, dry desert and the country suffers badly from bushfires almost every year. The fires are usually caused by lightning striking dry vegetation. Some species of trees found in Australia have adapted to cope with the constant outbreaks of fire. Eucalyptus trees can withstand fire, and some types of banksia trees actually need fire to open their seed pods.

Internet links

For links to websites with photo galleries, video clips and tours of Australasia and Oceania, go to **www.usborne-quicklinks.com**

These are the Palau Rock Islands of Micronesia, Oceania. There are over 200 rock islands in total. Each one is made of limestone rock and covered with thick forest.

Tropical islands

Lots of the small islands in the South Pacific are volcanoes. Coral reefs (dense colonies of tentacled sea animals) often grow in shallow waters around the islands. They form barriers which trap water between the reef and the island's coast. The trapped water is known as a lagoon.

Many of the volcanoes are inactive, and are slowly sinking back into the sea. Sometimes, a volcano sinks entirely into the sea, leaving behind a shallow lagoon surrounded by a coral reef. This is called an atoll.

This is Bora Bora Island, a volcanic island in the South Pacific. Vegetation is green, deep water is black and shallow water is pale blue.

The coral reef is the thin, white line around the edge.

This is Lake Eyre in Australia. It wasn't completely dry when this picture was taken – dry areas are pale pink and wet areas are dark pink.

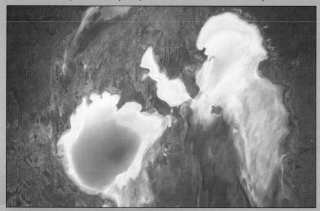

A vanishing lake

Australia's largest salt lake, Lake Eyre, is in the dry, central part of the country. Most of the year it is virtually dry, and you can see a glistening sheet of white salt on the lake bed. When the lake fills, it spreads out over 9,500 sq km (3,670 sq miles), but this usually only happens about once every eight years. The lake has two main sections, Lake Eyre North and Lake Eyre South, which are joined by a channel called the Goyder Channel.

Australasia and Oceania's attractions include a group of huge stone carvings, a strange tree formation and animals equipped with their own baby-carriers.

Great Barrier Reef

Around the coast of Queensland, Australia, lies the Great Barrier Reef, an enormous coral reef structure. It is made up of over 2,800 coral reefs, covering 345,000 sq km (133,200 sq miles) and is home to more than 1,500 species of fish.

Coral reefs are very fragile. They are found in clear, shallow waters with a constant, warm temperature. Global warming might make the sea too hot for coral reefs to survive, and the Great Barrier Reef could die out.

Easter Island

Easter Island is a remote island, far east of Australia, famous for its large stone carvings of human figures with large heads. The carvings are thought to be between 400 and 1,000 years old, and are believed to represent the spirits of important chiefs and ancestors of the island. A Dutch navigator named Jacob Roggeveen gave Easter Island its name when he first visited it on Easter day in 1722.

These sculptures on Easter Island were carved out of volcanic rock. They are about 4m (13ft) tall, and some are partly buried.

The Olgas

In Uluru National Park, in Australia's Northern Territory, there is a group of 36 enormous rocks known as the Olgas. The rocks are a type of sandstone, which means they were formed by loose sand that has become hardened and folded by the Earth's movements to produce layered rocks. The rocks were gradually eroded by wind and rain into the rounded hills we see today. The sand grains that make up the sandstone are mostly made of a pink mineral called feldspar.

These rounded rocks are the Olgas. The aboriginals, who were the first people to settle in Australia, named the site "Kata Tjunta" meaning "many heads".

This is a tree kangaroo, a type of animal only found in Queensland, Australia, and Papua New Guinea. Tree kangaroos can leap great distances from tree to tree.

Marsupials

Australasia and Oceania are home to lots of unusual animals, including a group of mammals called marsupials. As soon as marsupials are born, they crawl into a pouch of skin on their mother's tummy. They stay inside the pouch for the first few months of their lives. Kangaroos, koalas, wombats and possums are all marsupials.

The seven-in-one tree

On the island of Rarotonga, in the Cook Islands, there is a group of seven coconut trees which have grown naturally in a perfect circle. A legend tells that the seven trees grew from one seed, so they are known as the "seven-in-one tree", but they probably grew from seven separate seeds.

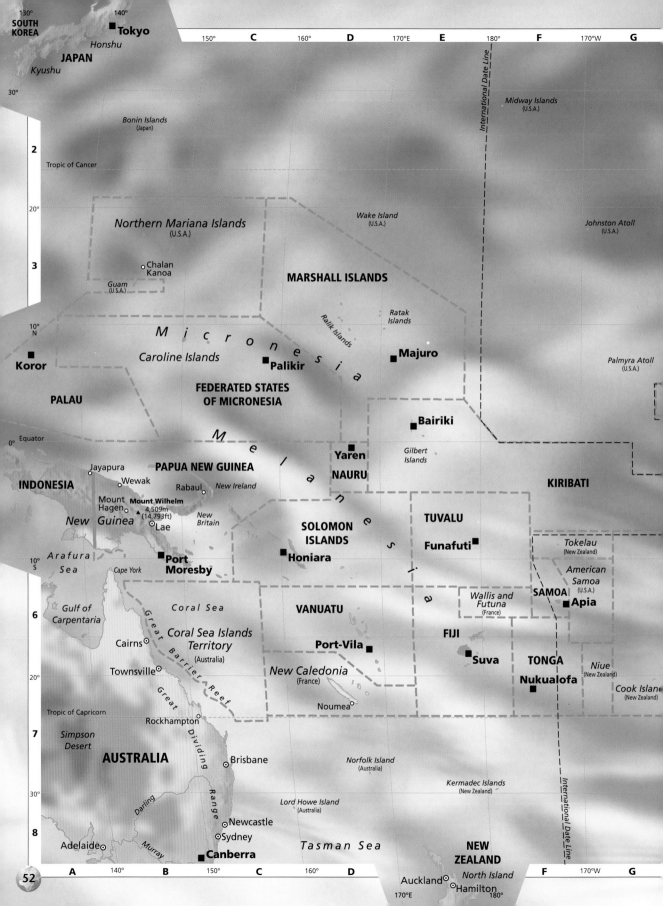

Tokyo

Honshu

JAPAN

Kyushu

30°

Bonin Islands
(Japan)

International Date Line

Midway Islands
(U.S.A.)

2

Tropic of Cancer

20°

Northern Mariana Islands
(U.S.A.)

Wake Island
(U.S.A.)

Johnston Atoll
(U.S.A.)

3

○ Chalan
Kanoa

Guam
(U.S.A.)

MARSHALL ISLANDS

10°
N

M i c r o n e s i a

Ralik Islands

Ratak Islands

■ **Majuro**

■
Koror

Caroline Islands

■ **Palikir**

Palmyra Atoll
(U.S.A.)

PALAU

**FEDERATED STATES
OF MICRONESIA**

*M
e
l
a
n
e
s
i
a*

■ **Bairiki**

0° Equator

Yaren ■

*Gilbert
Islands*

INDONESIA

Jayapura

PAPUA NEW GUINEA

NAURU

KIRIBATI

○ *Wewak*

New Ireland

○ *Rabaul*

New Britain

Mount
Hagen
Mount Wilhelm
▲ 4,509m
(14,793ft)
Lae

New Guinea

TUVALU

Tokelau
(New Zealand)

10°
S

*Arafura
Sea*

Cape York

■ **Port
Moresby**

**SOLOMON
ISLANDS**

■ **Honiara**

Funafuti ■

*American
Samoa*
(U.S.A.)

SAMOA

○ *Cairns*

Coral Sea

Great Barrier Reef

*Gulf of
Carpentaria*

*Coral Sea Islands
Territory*
(Australia)

VANUATU

*Wallis and
Futuna*
(France)

FIJI

■ **Apia**

6

○ *Townsville*

Port-Vila ■

New Caledonia
(France)

■ **Suva**

TONGA

Niue
(New Zealand)

20°

Noumea

■
Nukualofa

Cook Islands
(New Zealand)

Tropic of Capricorn

○ *Rockhampton*

7

*Simpson
Desert*

AUSTRALIA

○ *Brisbane*

Norfolk Island
(Australia)

Kermadec Islands
(New Zealand)

International Date Line

30°

Great Dividing Range

Darling

Lord Howe Island
(Australia)

8

○ *Newcastle*

○ *Sydney*

Adelaide ○

Murray

■ **Canberra**

Tasman Sea

**NEW
ZEALAND**

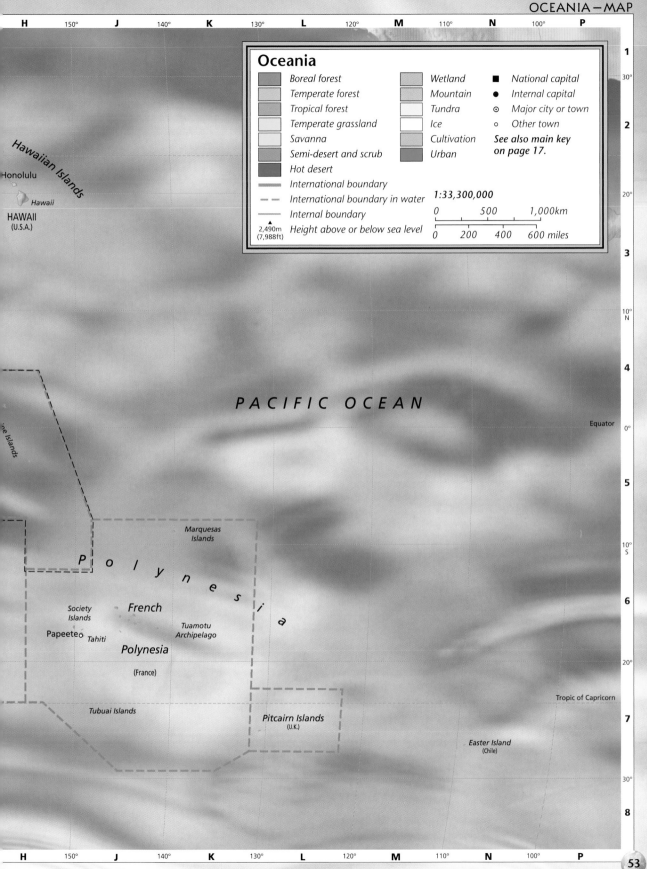

H 150° J 140° K 130° L 120° M 110° N 100° P

Oceania

Boreal forest		Wetland	■ National capital
Temperate forest		Mountain	● Internal capital
Tropical forest		Tundra	◉ Major city or town
Temperate grassland		Ice	○ Other town
Savanna		Cultivation	
Semi-desert and scrub		Urban	**See also main key**
Hot desert			**on page 17.**

International boundary
International boundary in water
Internal boundary
2,490m (7,988ft) Height above or below sea level

1:33,300,000

0	500	1,000km
0	200	400	600 miles

Hawaiian Islands

Honolulu

Hawaii

HAWAII
(U.S.A.)

PACIFIC OCEAN

Equator

ne Islands

Marquesas
Islands

P o l y n e s i a

Society
Islands

French

Papeete○ Tahiti

Tuamotu
Archipelago

Polynesia

(France)

Tubuai Islands

Pitcairn Islands
(U.K.)

Tropic of Capricorn

Easter Island
(Chile)

H 150° J 140° K 130° L 120° M 110° N 100° P

30°
20°
10° N
Equator 0°
10° S
20°
30°

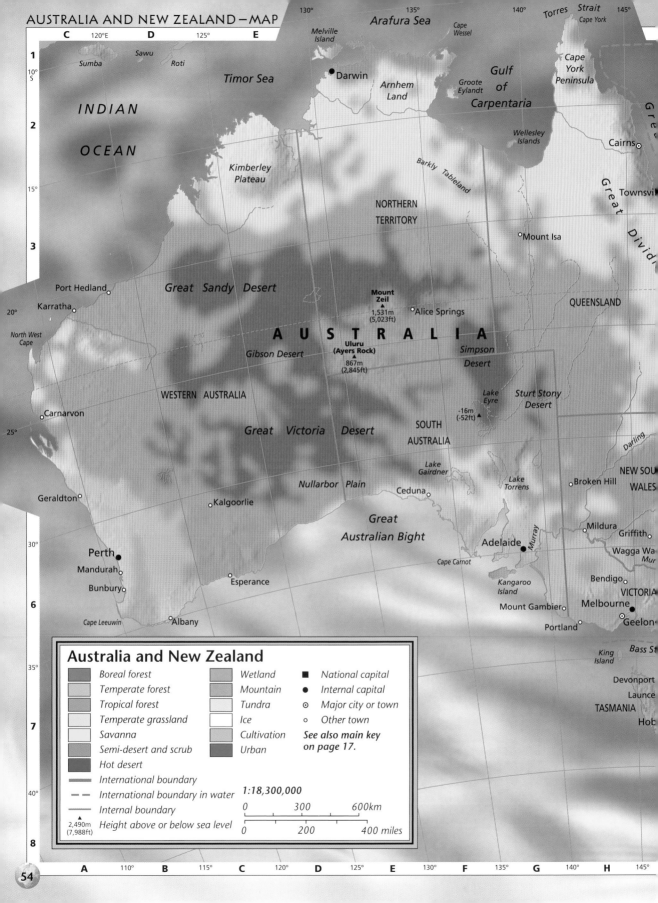

AUSTRALIA AND NEW ZEALAND—MAP

130° **Torres** Strait
135° 140° 145° Cape York

Arafura Sea

Cape Wessel

C 120°E D 125° E

1

10° S

Melville Island

Darwin

Timor Sea

Arnhem Land

Groote Eylandt

Gulf of Carpentaria

Cape York Peninsula

INDIAN

Wellesley Islands

Cairns

2

OCEAN

Kimberley Plateau

Barkly Tableland

Great Dividi

15°

NORTHERN TERRITORY

Townsvi

3

Port Hedland

Great Sandy Desert

Mount Isa

QUEENSLAND

20°

Karratha

Mount Zeil
▲
1,531m
(5,023ft)

Alice Springs

A U S T R A L I A

North West Cape

Gibson Desert

Uluru (Ayers Rock)
▲
867m
(2,845ft)

Simpson Desert

Carnarvon

WESTERN   AUSTRALIA

Lake Eyre

Sturt Stony Desert

25°

Great   Victoria   Desert

-16m
(-52ft) ▲

SOUTH AUSTRALIA

Darling

Nullarbor   Plain

Lake Gairdner

NEW SOU

Geraldton

Kalgoorlie

Ceduna

Lake Torrens

Broken Hill

WALES

30°

Perth

Mandurah

Bunbury

Esperance

Great Australian Bight

Cape Carnot

Adelaide

Murray

Mildura

Griffith

Wagga Wa

Mur

Bendigo

VICTORIA

Kangaroo Island

Melbourne

6

Cape Leeuwin

Albany

Mount Gambier

Portland

Geelon

King Island

Bass St

35°

Australia and New Zealand

Boreal forest	Wetland	■ National capital
Temperate forest	Mountain	● Internal capital
Tropical forest	Tundra	⊙ Major city or town
Temperate grassland	Ice	○ Other town
Savanna	Cultivation	*See also main key*
Semi-desert and scrub	Urban	*on page 17.*
Hot desert		

International boundary

International boundary in water

Internal boundary

▲ 2,490m (7,988ft) Height above or below sea level

1:18,300,000

0   300   600km

0   200   400 miles

Devonport

Launce

TASMANIA

Hob

7

40°

8

A 110° B 115° C 120° D 125° E 130° F 135° G 140° H 145°

ASIA

The shading on this map is there to help you see clearly the different countries that make up the continent.

Asia is the largest continent and has over 40 countries, including Russia, the biggest country in the world. As well as large land masses, it has thousands of islands and inlets, giving it over 160,000km (100,000 miles) of coastline. Turkey and Russia are partly in Europe and partly in Asia, but both are shown in full on the map on the right.

This is a type of Chinese boat called a junk, sailing in the sea off Singapore.

ARCTIC OCEAN

Franz Josef Land

Novaya Zemlya

Barents Sea

Kara Se

Ob

■ Moscow

R U S

Volga

Black Sea

■ Ankara
TURKEY

GEORGIA

■ Astana

KAZAKHSTAN

CYPRUS

ARMENIA

Caspian Sea

Aral Sea

AZERBAIJAN

UZBEKISTAN

LEBANON
Beirut■ **Syria**
■**Damascus**

TURKMENISTAN

Tashkent■

■**Bishkek**
KYRGYZSTAN

Jerusalem■
ISRAEL

■**Amman**
JORDAN

Ashgabat■

Dushanbe■

■**Baghdad**

■ **Tehran**

TAJIKISTAN

IRAQ

IRAN

Tropic of Cancer

KUWAIT

Kabul
AFGHANISTAN

■**Islamabad**

SAUDI ARABIA

BAHRAIN
QATAR

PAKISTAN

Indus

Riyadh■
Doha■

■**Abu Dhabi**

UNITED ARAB
EMIRATES

■ **Muscat**

New Delhi■

■**NEPAL**
Kathmandu

■**Thimp**
BANGLADE

Ganges

■**Sana**
YEMEN

OMAN

Arabian Sea

INDIA

*Socotra
(Yemen)*

*Bay of
Benga*

INDIAN OCEAN

Equator

Sri Jayewardenepura Kotte■

■**SRI LANKA**

■**Colombo**

MALDIVES
■**Male**

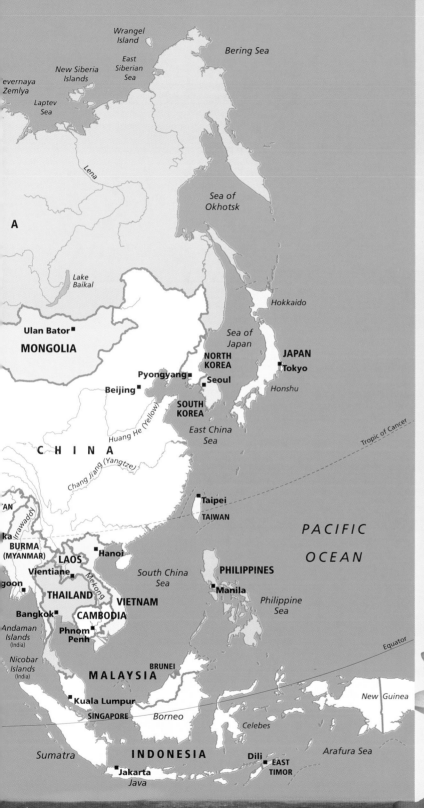

Wrangel
Island

Bering Sea

East
Siberian
Sea

New Siberia
Islands

evernaya
Zemlya

Laptev
Sea

Lena

A

Sea of
Okhotsk

Lake
Baikal

Hokkaido

Ulan Bator■

Sea of
Japan

MONGOLIA

NORTH
KOREA

JAPAN
■Tokyo

Pyongyang■

Seoul

Beijing■

Honshu

Huang He (Yellow)

SOUTH
KOREA

C H I N A

East China
Sea

Chang Jiang (Yangtze)

Tropic of Cancer

■Taipei

TAIWAN

PACIFIC

AN

OCEAN

(Irrawaddy)

ka

BURMA
(MYANMAR)

Hanoi■

LAOS

PHILIPPINES

Vientiane■

South China
Sea

■Manila

goon

THAILAND

VIETNAM

Philippine
Sea

Mekong

Bangkok■

CAMBODIA

Andaman
Islands
(India)

Phnom
Penh■

Equator

Nicobar
Islands
(India)

BRUNEI

MALAYSIA

New Guinea

■Kuala Lumpur

SINGAPORE

Borneo

Celebes

Sumatra

INDONESIA

Dili
■EAST
TIMOR

Arafura Sea

Jakarta■

Java

Facts

Total land area 44,537,920 sq km (17,196,090 sq miles)

Total population 3.8 billion (including all of Russia)

Biggest city Tokyo, Japan

Biggest country Russia *Total area: 17,075,200 sq km (6,592,735 sq miles) Area of Asiatic Russia: 12,780,800 sq km (4,934,667 sq miles)*

Smallest country Maldives *300 sq km (116 sq miles)*

Highest mountain Mount Everest, Nepal/China border *8,850m (29,035ft)*

Longest river Chang Jiang (Yangtze), China *6,380km (3,964 miles)*

Biggest lake Caspian Sea, western Asia *370,999 sq km (143,243 sq miles)*

Highest waterfall Jog Falls, on the Sharavati River, India *253m (830ft)*

Biggest desert Arabian Desert, in and around Saudi Arabia *2,230,000 sq km (900,000 sq miles)*

Biggest island Borneo *751,100 sq km (290,000 sq miles)*

Main mineral deposits Zinc, mica, tin, chromium, iron, nickel

Main fuel deposits Oil, coal, uranium, natural gas

These are lotus flowers, a type of water lily. In China they are associated with purity and for Buddhists they are sacred.

Asia is made up of all kinds of rugged terrain. In the far north are vast, frozen plains, and farther south are dry deserts. Asia also has enormous mountain ranges, including the Himalayas, the world's highest range. Most of Asia's population lives in the far south, which is hot and humid, with lush rainforests.

The white areas in the middle of this satellite image of Asia are mountain ranges, which include the Himalayas.

Empty land

Southern Saudi Arabia has a sandy desert that covers an area about the size of France. It is called Rub al Khali, and is often nicknamed the Empty Quarter as it has hardly any plants or animals and no permanent human settlements. Strong winds blow the sand into mounds that can be more than 330m (1,000ft) high, taller than the Eiffel Tower in Paris.

This view of Rub al Khali in Saudi Arabia shows how the wind has blown sand into long, high ridges.

This photograph shows a section of the Great Wall of China, which winds across northern China. The wall can be seen from space as a long, thin line.

This satellite image shows several volcanoes in Kamchatka, Russia. Red areas indicate snow. The pale streaks down the craters' sides are mudflows of ash and melting snow.

Russian wilderness

Kamchatka, in the far east of Russia, is one of the world's most remote areas. Its one main town is accessible only by air or sea. Much of the land is mountainous, with more than 300 volcanoes. Some of these are active, and they regularly eject boiling rivers of mud and great plumes of steam from their rocky craters.

Internet links

For links to websites where you can take a virtual tour of the Great Wall of China and see the River Ganges from space, go to **www.usborne-quicklinks.com**

A sacred river

The River Ganges begins in the Himalayas and flows through India and Bangladesh to the Indian Ocean. The river is regarded as holy by followers of the Hindu religion. Every day thousands of Hindus bathe in the Ganges, which they believe washes away their sins. People often worship the river by throwing flowers into it or floating oil lamps on its surface.

Here is the Ganges Delta in India, where the River Ganges flows into the Bay of Bengal (bottom).

Much of central and southern Asia is densely populated, so there are many large cities, including Tokyo, the world's most populous city. There are beautiful natural areas too, such as the forests and mountain ranges of China.

A panda climbs a tree in China. Pandas are good climbers, and often rest or sleep high in trees.

Pandas of China

Wild pandas live in the mountainous forests of China. Pandas depend on the bamboo that grows there, as their diet consists almost exclusively of bamboo shoots. But forests are being cut down, so pandas are losing their habitat and food source. There may be as few as 1,000 wild pandas left.

A floating market

Near Bangkok, in Thailand, there is a famous floating market which is held on a canal. Farmers go there daily with fresh fruit and vegetables piled high on narrow boats. Customers weave their way along the busy canal in similar boats, looking for bargains. They must come early, though, as the market begins at about 8 a.m., and everything is sold by 11 a.m.

These women have brought fruit and vegetables to sell at Bangkok's floating market.

Enormous department stores with glaring neon signs line a street in central Tokyo.

Japanese capital

One of Asia's most vibrant cities is Tokyo, the capital of Japan. This big, sprawling city has been rebuilt twice, first in the 1920s when an earthquake destroyed vast areas, and then after the Second World War, when bombs devastated the city. Modern Tokyo is a mixture of a few old streets and many new, towering skyscrapers.

Forbidden City

In the middle of the city of Beijing, in China, is an ancient, walled city. For hundreds of years it was the palace of China's kings, or emperors. It was known as the Forbidden City because no one but the emperor, his family and guests was allowed in its grounds.

China no longer has a royal family, and the Forbidden City is a popular tourist attraction. The city has 800 buildings, including huge temples and elaborate arches, decorated with ornate carvings and grand bronze statues.

Internet links

For links to websites where you can see panoramic movies of China's Forbidden City and take a tour of Tokyo, go to
www.usborne-quicklinks.com

This bronze tortoise stands in Beijing's Forbidden City. According to ancient Chinese beliefs, tortoises were divine animals, and tortoise statues were said to bring good luck.

The countries of western Asia are full of important cultural and historical sights, such as places of worship and the remains of ancient civilizations. The Asian part of Russia stretches far across the continent. It is dominated by the region of Siberia, where the climate is so harsh that most of the land is uninhabited.

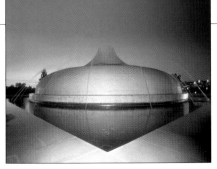

This museum in Jerusalem, Israel, houses ancient manuscripts known as the Dead Sea Scrolls.

The Dead Sea

The Dead Sea, in Israel, gets its name because it is so salty that nothing can live in it. However, many people swim in the sea, as its water contains health-giving minerals.

The Dead Sea is also famous for the Dead Sea Scrolls. These are 2,000-year-old Jewish handwritten papers that were discovered in caves by the sea. The scrolls cover mainly religious topics, and have helped historians to learn what life was like in ancient times.

Homes of rock

The region of Cappadocia, near Ankara in central Turkey, has a strange landscape of rocky cones, made of soft volcanic rock. Many hundreds of years ago, people carved caves in the rock, creating whole towns and villages that included houses, stables and even churches. They also built an amazing network of underground tunnels that linked the houses.

These rocky peaks in Cappadocia, Turkey, were carved out to create rock houses. Today, they are crumbling away.

Holy places

Many different religions are followed in Asia, and their various places of worship and study, such as Muslim mosques and Hindu temples, are found in towns and cities all over the continent. Many of these buildings are intricately decorated, for example with huge domes covered in thousands of patterned tiles.

This is the Trans-Siberian Express in Siberia. The train runs from Moscow to Vladivostok, stopping at other stations on the way.

This elaborate, domed building in Esfahan, Iran, is a school for Muslim students.

Russian train trip

Crossing the enormous country of Russia is the Trans-Siberian rail line. This is the longest rail line in the world, running more than 9,000km (5,600 miles) between Moscow in the west and Vladivostok in the east. The line passes through the plains of Siberia, which freeze over in winter. The fastest train trip along the line takes about seven days.

Reindeers

Siberia is home to many reindeers. They have thick fur that keeps them warm in winter, and also have such a good sense of smell that they can sniff out plants to eat that are buried deep under the snow.

Internet links

For links to websites where you can find sightseeing guides to the countries of Asia and climb a Buddhist temple, go to **www.usborne-quicklinks.com**

These reindeers are being driven by Siberian herders through western Siberia. Reindeers can easily pull heavy, loaded sleds.

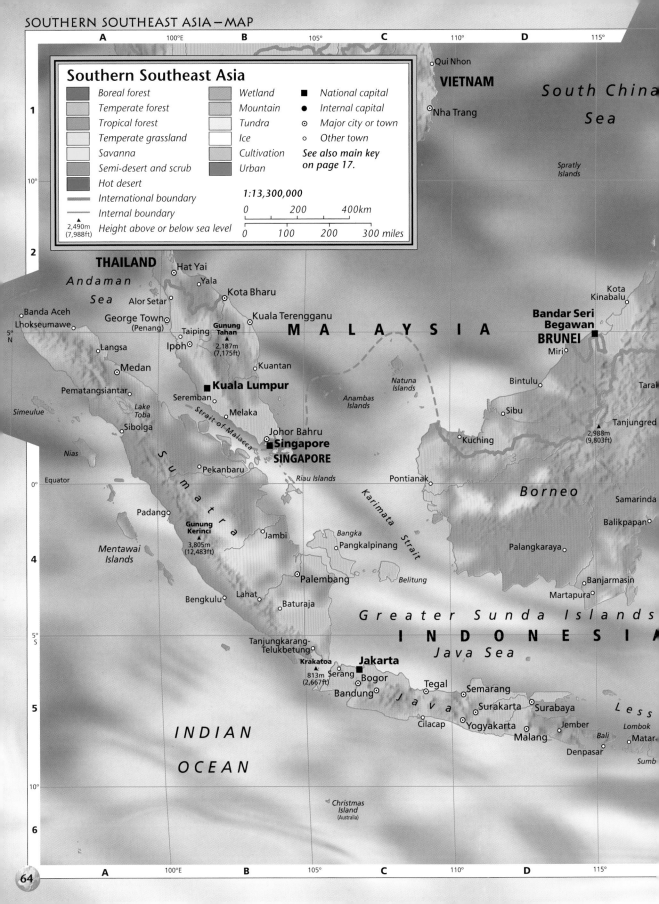

A 100°E B 105° C 110° D 115°

Southern Southeast Asia

- Boreal forest
- Temperate forest
- Tropical forest
- Temperate grassland
- Savanna
- Semi-desert and scrub
- Hot desert
- International boundary
- Internal boundary
▲ 2,490m (7,988ft) Height above or below sea level

- Wetland
- Mountain
- Tundra
- Ice
- Cultivation
- Urban

- ■ National capital
- ● Internal capital
- ⊙ Major city or town
- ○ Other town

See also main key on page 17.

1:13,300,000

0   200   400km

0   100   200   300 miles

Qui Nhon
VIETNAM
South China
Sea
Nha Trang

*Spratly
Islands*

THAILAND
*Andaman
Sea*
Hat Yai
Yala
Banda Aceh
Lhokseumawe
Alor Setar
Kota Bharu
George Town
(Penang)
Kuala Terengganu
M A L A Y S I A
Kota
Kinabalu
**Bandar Seri
Begawan**
BRUNEI
Taiping
Langsa
Ipoh
**Gunung
Tahan**
▲
2,187m
(7,175ft)
Kuantan
Miri
Medan
Bintulu
Taral
Pematangsiantar
Kuala Lumpur
*Natuna
Islands*
Sibu
Tanjungred
▲
2,988m
(9,803ft)
Seremban
*Anambas
Islands*
*Lake
Toba*
Melaka
Kuching
Simeulue
Strait of Malacca
Johor Bahru
Singapore
SINGAPORE
Pontianak
Borneo
Sibolga
Pekanbaru
Riau Islands
Samarinda
Nias
Equator
0°
Karimata Strait
Padang
**Gunung
Kerinci**
▲
3,805m
(12,483ft)
Jambi
Bangka
Balikpapan
*Mentawai
Islands*
Pangkalpinang
Palangkaraya
Bengkulu
Lahat
Palembang
Belitung
Banjarmasin
Baturaja
Martapura
G r e a t e r   S u n d a   I s l a n d s
5°S
Tanjungkarang-
Telukbetung
I N D O N E S I A
Java Sea
Krakatoa
▲
813m
(2,667ft)
Jakarta
Serang
Bogor
Tegal
Semarang
L e s s
Bandung
Surakarta
Surabaya
Lombok
INDIAN
Cilacap
Yogyakarta
Jember
Bali
Matar
Malang
Denpasar
Sumb
OCEAN
*Christmas
Island
(Australia)*

5°
N

10°

64

A 100°E B 105° C 110° D 115°

120° Cabanatuan 125°
Olongapo *Luzon*
Manila ■ Quezon City
Lucena
Calapan Naga
Mindoro Legaspi
PHILIPPINES
Masbate
Masbate
Roxas
Panay *Samar*
Calbayog
Taytay Iloilo Bacolod Tacloban
Calamian Group
Cebu
Philippine Sea
Negros *Bohol*
Puerto Princesa Surigao
Dumaguete Butuan
awan Cagayan de Oro
Sulu Sea Pagadian Iligan
Mindanao
dakan Zamboanga Davao
Jolo General Santos
Sulu Archipelago
au

Inset map

J 140°E K 145° L 150° M Equator 155° N
Jayapura *Admiralty Islands* **PACIFIC OCEAN**
4 Wewak *Bismarck Sea* *New Ireland* 4
5°S Rabaul
Mount Wilhelm 4,509m (14,793ft) ▲ Madang *New Britain* 5°S
Mount Hagen Lae
PAPUA NEW GUINEA
New Guinea Kerema *Solomon Sea*
5 5
Gulf of Papua D'Entrecasteaux *Islands*
10° **Port Moresby** ■ 10°
Torres Strait **1:20,000,000**
Cape York 0 400km
6 *Cape York Peninsula* 6
AUSTRALIA 0 200 miles
J 140°E K 145° L 150° M 155° N

Talaud Islands
PACIFIC **PALAU**
5°N
Celebes Sea **OCEAN**
Sangihe Islands
Morotai 3
Manado *Biak*
Ternate *Halmahera*
Gorontalo Sorong *Yapen*
Molucca Sea Equator 0°
Peleng Obi *Misool*
Palu
Celebes *Sula Islands* *Ceram Sea* Fakfak Jayapura
Palopo *Buru* *Ceram* *Puncak Jaya* *Maoke Range*
repare Kendari Ambon 5,030m (16,502ft) ▲ *New*
Watampone *Buton* *Guinea*
Ujung Pandang *Banda Sea* *Aru Islands* 5°S
Flores Sea
nda Islands *Wetar* *Tanimbar Islands* *Dolak*
Flores
Ende ■ **Dili**
Sumba **EAST TIMOR** *Arafura Sea* *Torres Strait*
Sawu *Timor*
Sawu Sea Kupang 10°
Roti
Timor Sea **AUSTRALIA** 6
● Darwin **NORTHERN TERRITORY**
120° F 125° G 130° H 135° J 140°

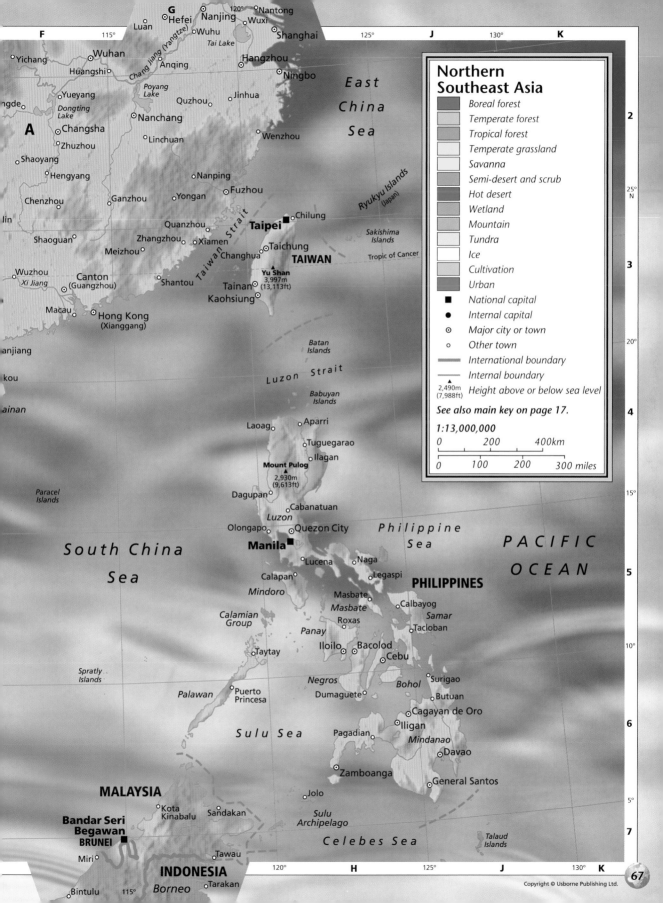

Northern
Southeast Asia

Boreal forest
Temperate forest
Tropical forest
Temperate grassland
Savanna
Semi-desert and scrub
Hot desert
Wetland
Mountain
Tundra
Ice
Cultivation
Urban
■ National capital
● Internal capital
⊙ Major city or town
○ Other town
— International boundary
— Internal boundary
▲ 2,490m
(7,988ft) Height above or below sea level

See also main key on page 17.

1:13,000,000

| 0 | 200 | 400km |
| 0 | 100 | 200 | 300 miles |

East
China
Sea

Yichang
Wuhan
Huangshi
Yueyang
Dongting Lake
Changsha
Zhuzhou
Shaoyang
Hengyang
Chenzhou
Jin
Shaoguan
Wuzhou
Canton
(Guangzhou)
Xi Jiang
Macau
Hong Kong
(Xianggang)
Hefei
Luan
Nanjing
Wuhu
Anqing
Nanchang
Poyang Lake
Quzhou
Linchuan
Ganzhou
Yongan
Nanping
Fuzhou
Quanzhou
Zhangzhou
Meizhou
Xiamen
Shantou
Nantong
Wuxi
Shanghai
Hangzhou
Ningbo
Jinhua
Wenzhou
Chang Jiang (Yangtze)
Tai Lake

Ryukyu Islands (Japan)
Sakishima Islands
Tropic of Cancer

Taipei ■ Chilung
Taichung
Changhua
TAIWAN
Yu Shan 3,997m (13,113ft)
Tainan
Kaohsiung
Taiwan Strait

anjiang
kou
ainan

Paracel Islands

South China
Sea

Spratly Islands

Batan Islands

Luzon Strait

Babuyan Islands

Laoag
Aparri
Tuguegarao
Ilagan
Mount Pulog ▲ 2,930m (9,613ft)
Dagupan
Cabanatuan
Luzon
Olongapo
Quezon City
Manila ■
Lucena
Naga
Legaspi
Calapan
Mindoro
Masbate
Masbate
Roxas
Panay
Iloilo
Bacolod
Cebu
Taytay
Negros
Dumaguete
Bohol
Surigao
Butuan
Cagayan de Oro
Iligan
Mindanao
Davao
Zamboanga
General Santos

Philippine Sea

PHILIPPINES

PACIFIC
OCEAN

Calbayog
Samar
Tacloban

Calamian Group

Puerto Princesa
Palawan

Sulu Sea

Pagadian

Jolo
Sulu Archipelago

Celebes Sea

Talaud Islands

MALAYSIA
Bandar Seri Begawan ■
BRUNEI
Kota Kinabalu
Sandakan
Tawau
Miri
INDONESIA
Borneo
Bintulu
Tarakan

67

Copyright © Usborne Publishing Ltd.

A 80°E B 85° C 90° D 95° E 100° F 105° G 110°

KAZAKHSTAN

Almaty Karamay

Lake
Issyk Yining Kuytun *Dzungarian
Basin* Altay Altay Bulgan

Ulan Bator

KYRGYZSTAN Shihezi

Pik Pobedy
7,439m
(24,406ft) Urumqi *T i e n   S h a n* **MONGOLIA**

Aksu Turpan *Bosten
Lake* -154m
(-505ft) Hami

40°
N Korla *Turpan
Depression*

G o b i   D e s e r t Eren

Tarim Basin Lop Lake Baotou Hohh

35° Hotan *Taklimakan
Desert* Mogao Caves *The Great Wall of China* Wuhai

Altun Mountains Yumen 5,547m
(18,199ft) Yinchuan

Kunlun Mountains *Qaidam
Basin* Golmud *Qinghai
Lake* Xining Lanzhou Taiy

4 *Huang He (Yellow)* **CHINA** Baoji Mount Li
(Terracotta

Plateau of Tibet Xian

30° *Siling Lake* Yushu Shiyan

TIBET *Chang Jiang (Yangtze)* Xiang

Himalayas *Nam Lake* *Salween* *Mekong* Chengdu Yichang

5 **NEPAL** **Kathmandu** *Brahmaputra* Lhasa Gongga Shan
7,556m
(24,790ft) Leshan Chongqing Changd

Mount Everest
8,850m
(29,035ft) Darjeeling **Thimphu** Luzhou

Darbhanga Biratnagar **BHUTAN** *Chang Jiang (Yangtze)* Zunyi Huaihua

25° Patna *Ganges* *Brahmaputra* Dibrugarh Xichang Heng

Bhagalpur Rangpur Guwahati Panzhihua Guiyang

INDIA Shillong Dali

Ranchi Asansol Rajshahi Sylhet *Irrawaddy* Kunming Guilin

Tropic of Cancer **BANGLADESH** Imphal Myitkyina

6 **Dhaka** Aizawl Liuzhou

Kolkata
(Calcutta) Khulna Lashio *Red* Gejiu Nanning Wuzhou

Chittagong Monywa Mandalay Simao Lao Cai Yulin

Cuttack *Mouths of the
Ganges* Mount
Victoria
3,053m
(10,016ft) **BURMA
(MYANMAR)** Phongsali Son La Thai
Nguyen Zhanji

Bay of Bengal Sittwe Taunggyi **Hanoi**

20° Pyinmana *Mekong* Hai
Phong Haikou

7 *INDIAN* Sandoway Pye *Salween* Louangphrabang *Gulf of
Tonkin* Haina

OCEAN Chiang
Mai **LAOS** Thanh Hoa **VIETNAM**

Henzada *Irrawaddy* **THAILAND** **Vientiane** Vinh

Pathein Pegu Udon Thani Sanya

15° **Rangoon**

*Mouths of the
Irrawaddy* Moulmein 100° 105° 110°

C 90°E D 95° F G

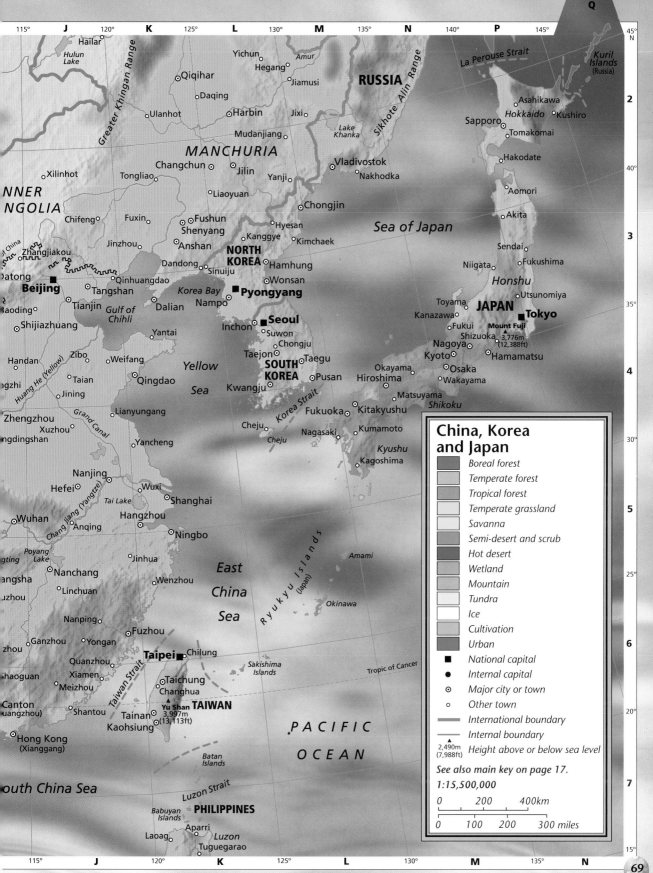

115° **J** 120° **K** 125° **L** 130° **M** 135° **N** 140° **P** 145° 45°
N

Hailar

Hulun Lake

Qiqihar
Yichun
Hegang
Jiamusi
Amur

Daqing

RUSSIA

Sikhote Alin Range

La Perouse Strait

Kuril Islands (Russia)

2

Asahikawa
Kushiro

Hokkaido
Sapporo
Tomakomai

Ulanhot
Harbin
Jixi

Mudanjiang

Hakodate

Changchun
Jilin
Vladivostok
Nakhodka

MANCHURIA

Xilinhot
NNER NGOLIA

Tongliao
Liaoyuan
Yanji

Aomori

40°

Chifeng
Fuxin
Fushun
Shenyang
Chongjin

Akita

3

Jinzhou
Anshan
Hyesan
Kanggye
Kimchaek

Sea of Japan

Sendai
Fukushima

Gulf of China
Zhangjiakou
Qinhuangdao
Dandong
Sinuiju

NORTH KOREA
Hamhung

Niigata

Honshu

Datong
Beijing
Tangshan
Dalian
Wonsan

Utsunomiya

Toyama
JAPAN

35°

Baoding
Tianjin
Gulf of Chihli

Korea Bay
Nampo
■ **Pyongyang**

Kanazawa
Fukui
Shizuoka

Tokyo

Mount Fuji 3,776m (12,388ft)

Shijiazhuang
Yantai
Inchon
■ **Seoul**
Suwon

Nagoya
Kyoto
Hamamatsu

Handan
Zibo
Weifang
Chongju

Osaka
Wakayama

4

Taian
Qingdao
Taejon
Taegu

Okayama
Hiroshima

ngzhi
Jining

SOUTH KOREA
Pusan

Matsuyama

Zhengzhou
Xuzhou
Grand Canal
Lianyungang
Yellow Sea
Kwangju

Fukuoka
Kitakyushu

Shikoku

ngdingshan
Yancheng
Cheju
Korea Strait
Nagasaki
Kumamoto

30°

Cheju

Huang He (Yellow)

Nanjing
Hefei
Wuxi

Tai Lake
Shanghai
Kyushu
Kagoshima

5

Wuhan
Anqing
Hangzhou

Chang Jiang (Yangtze)

Amami

Poyang Lake
gting
Ningbo

Nanchang
Jinhua

East China Sea

R y u k y u   I s l a n d s (Japan)

Changsha
Linchuan
Wenzhou

Okinawa

25°

zhou
Nanping

Ganzhou
Yongan
Fuzhou

6

haoguan
Quanzhou
Xiamen
Taipei
Chilung

Sakishima Islands

Tropic of Cancer

Meizhou
Taichung
Changhua

Canton
Shantou
Yu Shan 3,997m (13,113ft)
TAIWAN

20°

uangzhou)
Tainan
Kaohsiung

P A C I F I C

Hong Kong (Xianggang)

Batan Islands

O C E A N

7

outh China Sea
Luzon Strait

Babuyan Islands
PHILIPPINES

Laoag
Aparri
Luzon
Tuguegarao

15°

115° **J** 120° **K** 125° **L** 130° **M** 135° **N**

China, Korea and Japan

▮	Boreal forest
▮	Temperate forest
▮	Tropical forest
▮	Temperate grassland
▮	Savanna
▮	Semi-desert and scrub
▮	Hot desert
▮	Wetland
▮	Mountain
▮	Tundra
▮	Ice
▮	Cultivation
▮	Urban
■	National capital
●	Internal capital
⊙	Major city or town
○	Other town
▬	International boundary
▬	Internal boundary
▲ 2,490m (7,988ft)	Height above or below sea level

See also main key on page 17.

1:15,500,000

0   200   400km

0   100   200   300 miles

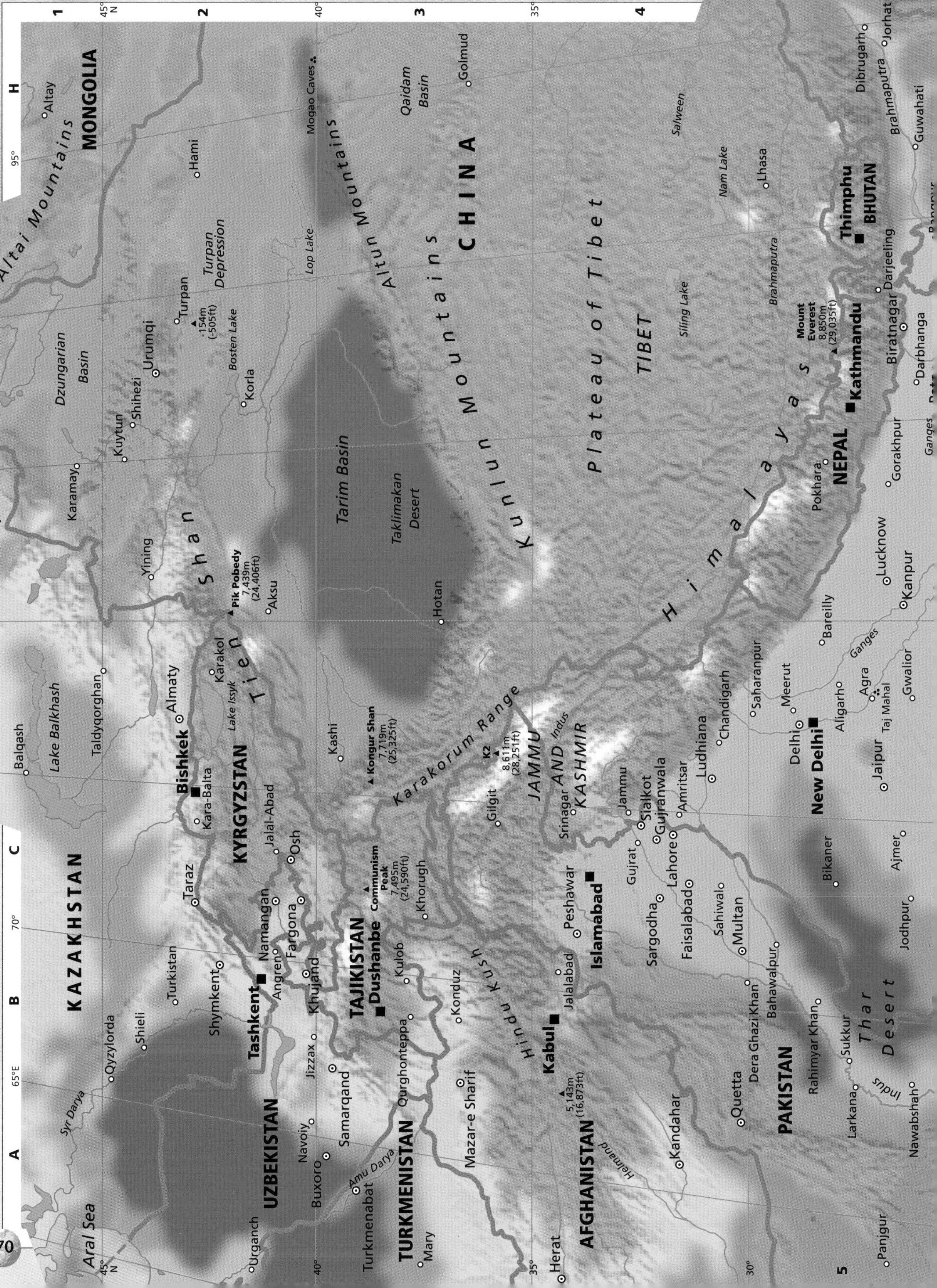
KAZAKHSTAN
UZBEKISTAN
TURKMENISTAN
KYRGYZSTAN
TAJIKISTAN
AFGHANISTAN
PAKISTAN
MONGOLIA
CHINA
TIBET
NEPAL
BHUTAN
JAMMU AND KASHMIR
Aral Sea
Lake Balkhash
Lake Issyk
Lake Zaysan
Bosten Lake
Lop Lake
Siling Lake
Nam Lake
Syr Darya
Amu Darya
Helmand
Indus
Ganges
Brahmaputra
Salween
Altai Mountains
Tien Shan
Kunlun Mountains
Altun Mountains
Karakorum Range
Hindu Kush
Himalayas
Plateau of Tibet
Tarim Basin
Taklimakan Desert
Dzungarian Basin
Turpan Depression
Qaidam Basin
Thar Desert
Mogao Caves
Taj Mahal
Pik Pobedy 7,439m (24,406ft)
Kongur Shan 7,719m (25,325ft)
Communism Peak 7,495m (24,590ft)
K2 8,611m (28,251ft)
Mount Everest 8,850m (29,035ft)
5,143m (16,873ft)
-154m (-505ft)
Tashkent
Bishkek
Dushanbe
Kabul
Islamabad
New Delhi
Kathmandu
Thimphu
Almaty
Urganch
Buxoro
Navoiy
Samarqand
Qyzylorda
Shieli
Turkistan
Shymkent
Taraz
Jizzax
Khujand
Angren
Namangan
Fargona
Jalal-Abad
Osh
Kara-Balta
Karakol
Taldyqorghan
Balqash
Turkmenabat
Mary
Qurghonteppa
Kulob
Khorugh
Konduz
Mazar-e Sharif
Herat
Kandahar
Jalalabad
Peshawar
Quetta
Dera Ghazi Khan
Bahawalpur
Rahimyar Khan
Sukkur
Larkana
Nawabshah
Panjgur
Multan
Sahiwal
Faisalabad
Sargodha
Gujrat
Lahore
Gujranwala
Sialkot
Jammu
Srinagar
Gilgit
Amritsar
Ludhiana
Chandigarh
Saharanpur
Meerut
Delhi
Aligarh
Agra
Gwalior
Jaipur
Ajmer
Jodhpur
Bikaner
Bareilly
Lucknow
Kanpur
Gorakhpur
Pokhara
Biratnagar
Darbhanga
Darjeeling
Guwahati
Dibrugarh
Jorhat
Lhasa
Kashi
Aksu
Hotan
Yining
Karamay
Kuytun
Shihezi
Urumqi
Korla
Turpan
Hami
Altay
Golmud
45° N
40°
35°
30°
65°E
70°
75°
80°
85°
90°
95°
A
B
C
H
1
2
3
4
5

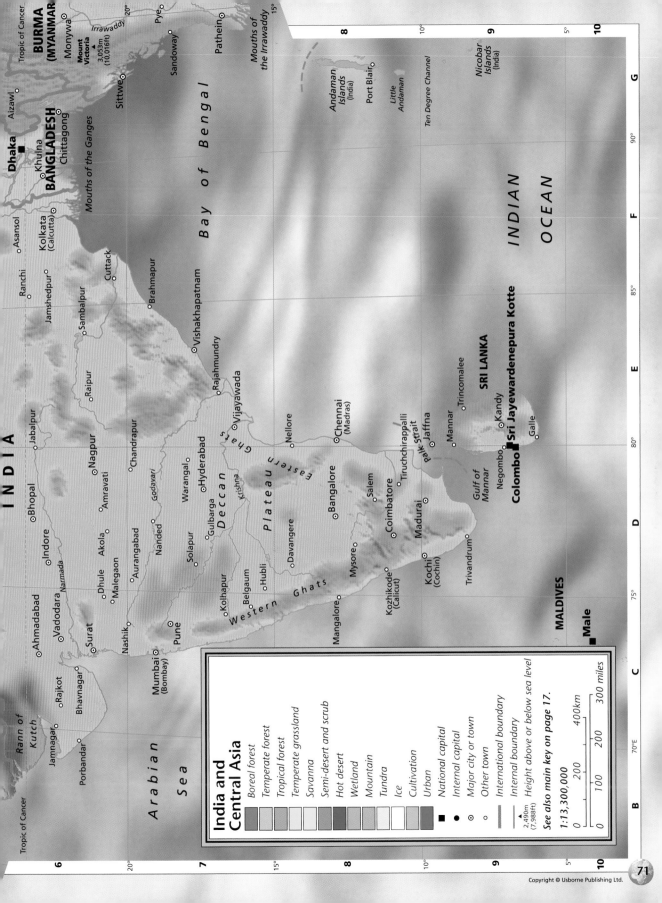

India and Central Asia

Boreal forest
Temperate forest
Tropical forest
Temperate grassland
Savanna
Semi-desert and scrub
Hot desert
Wetland
Mountain
Tundra
Ice
Cultivation
Urban

■ National capital
● Internal capital
⊙ Major city or town
○ Other town
— International boundary
— Internal boundary
▲ 2,490m (7,988ft) Height above or below sea level

See also main key on page 17.

1:13,300,000

0   100   200   400km
0   200   300 miles

INDIA

Tropic of Cancer

Rann of Kutch

Arabian Sea

Jamnagar
Porbandar
Rajkot
Bhavnagar
Ahmadabad
Vadodara
Surat
Mumbai (Bombay)
Nashik
Pune
Kolhapur
Belgaum
Hubli
Mangalore
Kozhikode (Calicut)
Dhule
Malegaon
Aurangabad
Solapur
Nanded
Gulbarga
Mysore
Kochi (Cochin)
Trivandrum

Jabalpur
Bhopal
Indore
Narmada
Akola
Amravati
Nagpur
Chandrapur
Godavari
Warangal
Hyderabad
Deccan
Krishna
Davangere
Plateau
Bangalore
Salem
Coimbatore
Madurai
Tiruchchirappalli

Western Ghats
Eastern Ghats

Ranchi
Jamshedpur
Sambalpur
Raipur
Brahmapur
Cuttack
Rajahmundry
Vijayawada
Nellore
Chennai (Madras)

BANGLADESH
Dhaka
Khulna
Chittagong
Asansol
Kolkata (Calcutta)

Mouths of the Ganges

BURMA (MYANMAR)
Monywa
Mount Victoria ▲ 3,053m (10,016ft)
Aizawl
Sittwe
Sandoway
Pye
Pathein
Mouths of the Irrawaddy
Irrawaddy

Bay of Bengal

Andaman Islands (India)
Port Blair
Little Andaman
Ten Degree Channel
Nicobar Islands (India)

SRI LANKA
Trincomalee
Jaffna
Mannar
Negombo
Kandy
Colombo ■ Sri Jayewardenepura Kotte
Galle
Palk Strait
Gulf of Mannar

MALDIVES
■ Male

INDIAN OCEAN

Tropic of Cancer

Copyright © Usborne Publishing Ltd.

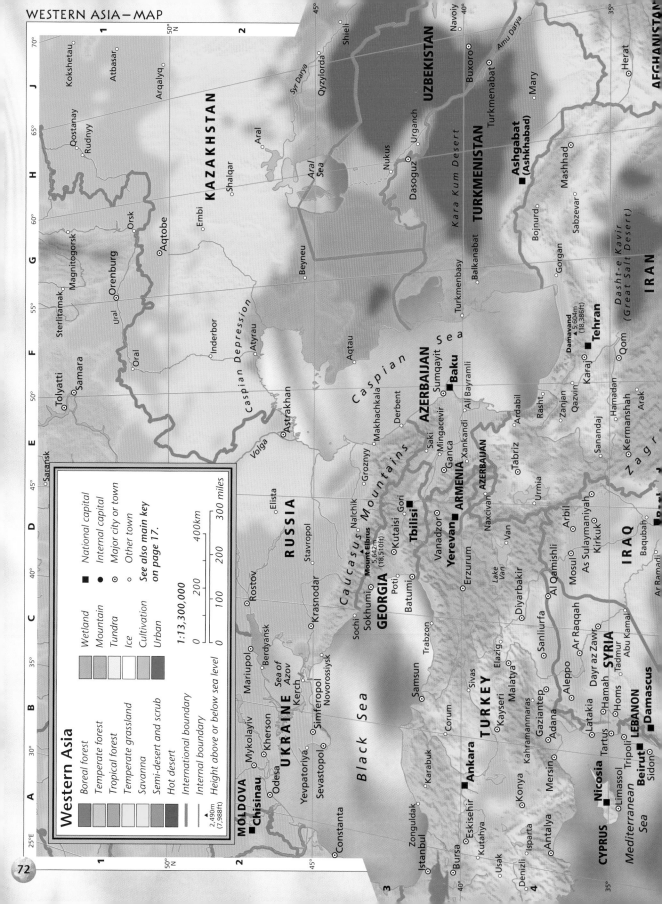

PAKISTAN

Helmand 30°

25° Turbat

Panjgur

Zabol

Iranshahr

Zahedan

Kerman

Sirjan

Bandar-e Abbas

Persepolis

Shiraz

Strait of Hormuz

Ahvaz

Mountains

Bushehr

Abadan

Busra

Al Amaran

Tigris

An Nasiriyah

Euphrates

Sur

Gulf of Oman

Tropic of Cancer

Suhar

Masirah Island

Muscat

OMAN

INDIAN

OCEAN

Arabian Sea

Socotra
(Yemen)

Cape Guardafui

Al Ayn

UNITED ARAB
EMIRATES

Dubai

Sharjah

Abu Dhabi

Salalah

Persian Gulf
(The Gulf)

Manama

BAHRAIN

Doha

QATAR

Kuwait City

KUWAIT

Ad Dammam

Al Mubarrez

Haradh

Arabian Peninsula

Rub al Khali
(Empty Quarter)

YEMEN

Hadhramaut

Al Mukalla

Gulf of Aden

SOMALIA

Riyadh

SAUDI ARABIA

Buraydah

Hail

Najran

Marib

Sadah

Dhamar

Ibb

Taizz

Aden

Berbera

Hargeysa
45°

50°

55°

60°

Syrian Desert

Medina

Mecca

At Taif

Asir

Abha

3,133m
(10,279ft)

Farasan
Islands

Sana

3,760m
(12,336ft)

Al Hudaydah

Bab al Mandab

Assab

Dikhil

DJIBOUTI

Djibouti

Amman

ISRAEL

JORDAN

Jerusalem

Gaza

Beer Sheva

Port Said

El Mansura

Ismailia

Suez Canal

Suez

Cairo

El Minya

Asyut

Sohag

Qena

Luxor

Valley of
the Kings

25°

Beni Suef

Pyramids of Giza

Nile

Aswan

Aswan High Dam

Tropic of Cancer

Lake
Nasser

EGYPT

Arabian

Desert

Nubian Desert

SUDAN

Atbarah

Wad Medani

Gedaref

Kassala

Teseney

ERITREA

Keren

Karora

Asmara

Massawa

Dahlak
Archipelago

Kobar
Sink
-116m
(-381ft)

Mekele

Ras Dashen
4,620m
(15,157ft)

Gonder

Bahir Dar

Lake Tana

Dese

ETHIOPIA

Ethiopian

Highlands

Blue Nile

Dire Dawa

35°E

40°

Port Sudan

Red

Sea

Hejaz

Jedda

Tabuk

Al Aqabah

Maan

Petra

Sharm el Sheikh

Hurghada

Elat

Sinai

Mount
Sinai
2,285m
(7,497ft)

Beer Sheva

Nile

30°N

35°

20°

6

7

8

9

H

G

F

7

8

9

73

Copyright © Usborne Publishing Ltd.

60° 2 80° A 1
20°
B
ARCTM
40° Franz Josef
Land
C
60°
D
80°

UNITED
KINGDOM
London
North
Sea
Norwegian
Sea
Arctic Circle
Svalbard
(Norway)

Paris
NETHERLANDS
BELGIUM
LUXEMBOURG
FRANCE
DENMARK
NORWAY
Oslo
SWEDEN
North Cape
Murmansk
Barents
Sea
Novaya
Zemlya

GERMANY
Berlin
Baltic
Sea
Stockholm
FINLAND
Kola
Peninsula
Kara
Sea

3
CZECH
REPUBLIC
AUSTRIA
POLAND
LITHUANIA
Warsaw
Vilnius
LATVIA
ESTONIA
Helsinki
Lake
Ladoga
St. Petersburg
Lake
Onega
Arkhangelsk
Vorkuta
Noril

SLOVAKIA
Budapest
HUNGARY
BELARUS
Minsk
Cherepovets
Ukhta

Lviv
Novyy Urengoy

ROMANIA
Kiev
MOLDOVA
Chisinau
UKRAINE
Moscow
Ryazan
Nizhniy Novgorod
Ural Mountains
Ob
West Siberian

Kharkiv
Voronezh
Volga
Kazan
Perm
Plain

Odesa
Dnipropetrovsk
Surgut
Ob
Yenisey

40°
N
Simferopol
Rostov
Samara
Yekaterinburg
R
U

Black
Sea
Volgograd
Krasnodar
Oral
Orenburg
Chelyabinsk
Irtysh
Omsk
Tomsk
Krasnoya

Ankara
Astrakhan
Aqtobe
Pavlodar
Novosibirsk

TURKEY
Mount Elbrus
5,642m
(18,510ft)
Atyrau
Barnaul
Ab

Adana
GEORGIA
Tbilisi
KAZAKHSTAN
Astana

Aleppo
ARMENIA
Yerevan
Aqtau
Qaraghandy
Uskemen
Kyz

SYRIA
AZERBAIJAN
Baku
Caspian Sea
Aral
Sea
Balqash
Altay

Mosul
Tabriz
Nukus
Qyzylorda
Lake
Balkhash
A

4
Baghdad
IRAQ
Damavand
5,604m
(18,386ft)
Tehran
Dasoguz
UZBEKISTAN
TURKMENISTAN
Shymkent
Almaty
Urumqi

Ahvaz
Esfahan
Turkmenabat
Ashgabat
(Ashkhabad)
Tashkent
Samarqand
Osh
Bishkek
KYRGYZSTAN
Tien Shan
Aksu

Mashhad
Dushanbe
TAJIKISTAN
Tarim Basin

Kuwait City
KUWAIT
IRAN
Herat
Mazar-e Sharif
Taklimakan Desert

SAUDI
ARABIA
Shiraz
Hotan

Riyadh
Manama
QATAR
Doha
Bandar-e
Abbas
Zahedan
AFGHANISTAN
Kabul
Kandahar
Islamabad
K2
8,611m
(28,251ft)
Srinagar

Abu Dhabi
Persian Gulf (The Gulf)
Indus
Lahore
PAKISTAN
INDIA
Plateau of Tibet

C 60°E D 80° E

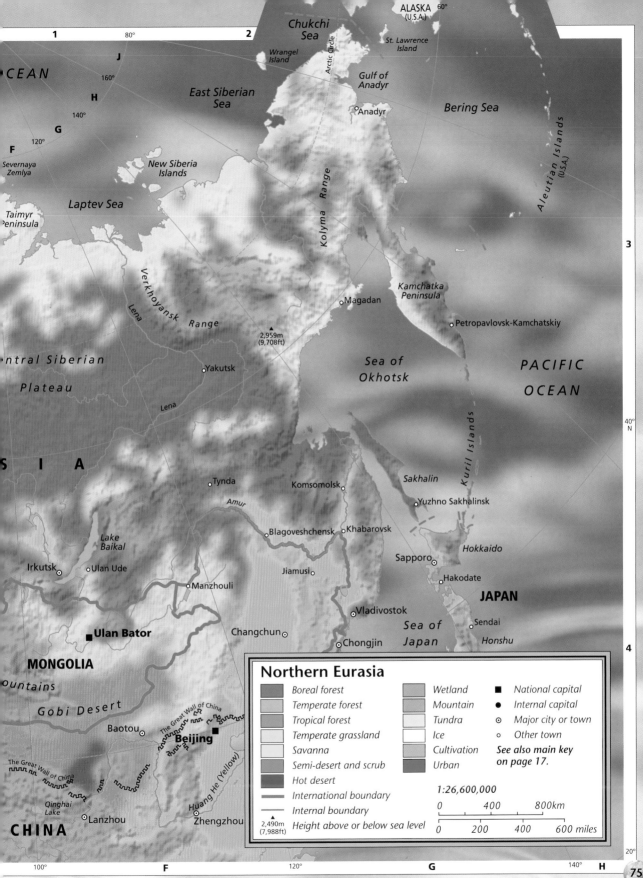

ALASKA 60°
(U.S.A.)

Chukchi
Sea

St. Lawrence
Island

Arctic Circle

J 160°

H 140°

G 120°

F

Severnaya
Zemlya

OCEAN

East Siberian
Sea

Wrangel
Island

Gulf of
Anadyr

Anadyr

Bering Sea

New Siberia
Islands

Aleutian Islands
(U.S.A.)

Taimyr
Peninsula

Laptev Sea

Kolyma Range

3

Verkhoyansk Range

Lena

Magadan

Kamchatka
Peninsula

Petropavlovsk-Kamchatskiy

PACIFIC

2,959m
(9,708ft)

ntral Siberian
Plateau

Yakutsk

Lena

Sea of
Okhotsk

OCEAN

40°
N

S I A

Tynda

Komsomolsk

Sakhalin

Kuril Islands

Amur

Yuzhno Sakhalinsk

Lake
Baikal

Blagoveshchensk

Khabarovsk

Hokkaido

Irkutsk

Ulan Ude

Jiamusi

Sapporo

Manzhouli

Hakodate

JAPAN

Vladivostok

Sendai

Changchun

Chongjin

Sea of
Japan

Honshu

4

Ulan Bator

MONGOLIA

ountains

Gobi Desert

The Great Wall of China

Baotou

Beijing

The Great Wall of China

Huang He (Yellow)

Qinghai
Lake

Lanzhou

Zhengzhou

CHINA

Northern Eurasia

Boreal forest	Wetland	National capital
Temperate forest	Mountain	Internal capital
Tropical forest	Tundra	Major city or town
Temperate grassland	Ice	Other town
Savanna	Cultivation	
Semi-desert and scrub	Urban	*See also main key on page 17.*
Hot desert		

International boundary

Internal boundary

2,490m
(7,988ft) Height above or below sea level

1:26,600,000

0   400   800km

0   200   400   600 miles

20°

100° F 120° G 140° H

75

Copyright © Usborne Publishing Ltd.

EUROPE

Europe is a small continent, packed with over 40 countries and more than 700 million people. Russia is an enormous country, spanning two continents. Its western part is in Europe, while its eastern part is in Asia. The European part of Russia is larger than any other country in Europe.

The shading on this map is there to help you see clearly the different countries that make up the continent.

ARCTIC OCEAN

Reykjavik
ICELAND

Norwegian
Sea

Faroe Islands
(Denmark)

SWEDEN

Shetland
Islands

NORWAY

Oslo

Orkney
Islands

Stockholm

North

Sea

DENMARK

Bal
Se

IRELAND
Dublin

Copenhagen

UNITED
KINGDOM

The
Hague

Amsterdam

London

Berlin

PO

NETHERLANDS

Brussels

GERMANY

BELGIUM

LUXEMBOURG

Paris

Luxembourg

Prague

CZECH
REPUBLIC

Rhine

Vienna

ATLANTIC

Bay
of
Biscay

FRANCE

SWITZERLAND

LIECHTENSTEIN

Bratislava

Bern

Vaduz

AUSTRIA

Budapes

OCEAN

SLOVENIA

HUNGA

Ljubljana

Zagreb

CROATI

MONACO

SAN MARINO

BOSNIA AND
HERZEGOVIN

ANDORRA

Sarajevo

PORTUGAL

Andorra
la Vella

ITALY

Lisbon

Madrid

Corsica

Rome

VATICAN CITY

SPAIN

ALBA
Tir

Balearic
Islands

Sardinia

Mediterranean Sea

Sicily

MALTA
Valletta

Barents Sea

Murmansk

Arkhangelsk

FINLAND

RUSSIA

sinki

Tallinn
ESTONIA

St. Petersburg

iga   LATVIA

Nizhniy Novgorod   Kazan

Moscow

THUANIA
Vilnius

A

Minsk

Volga

BELARUS

arsaw

Kiev   Volgograd

Dnieper

UKRAINE

VAKIA

MOLDOVA

Chisinau

ROMANIA

grade

Bucharest   Black Sea

Danube

OSLAVIA

BULGARIA

Sofia

Skopje

CEDONIA   TURKEY

EECE

Athens

Crete

Facts

Total land area 10,205,720 sq km (3,940,428 sq miles) (including European Russia)

Total population 727 million (including all of Russia)

Biggest city Moscow, Russia

Biggest country Russia *Total area: 17,075,200 sq km (6,592,735 sq miles) Area of European Russia: 4,294,400 sq km (1,658,068 sq miles)*

Smallest country Vatican City *0.44 sq km (0.17 sq miles)*

Highest mountain Elbrus, Russia *5,642m (18,510ft)*

Longest river Volga *3,700km (2,298 miles)*

Biggest lake Lake Ladoga, Russia *17,700 sq km (6,834 sq miles)*

Highest waterfall Utigard, on the Jostedal Glacier, Norway *800m (2,625ft)*

Biggest desert No deserts in Europe

Biggest island Great Britain *234,410 sq km (90,506 sq miles)*

Main mineral deposits Bauxite, zinc, iron, potash, fluorspar

Main fuel deposits Oil, coal, natural gas, peat, uranium

A cow in Devon, in the south of England

Europe has lots of islands and many of its countries are largely surrounded by sea. The Alps, one of Europe's principal mountain ranges, lies in the west, and is the source of many of its major rivers, including the Rhine and the Rhone.

This is a satellite image of Mount Vesuvius, a volcano in southern Italy. The black dot in the middle is the crater.

Europe by night

Satellite pictures taken at night show how much light is being generated in different areas. Highly populated areas, such as Europe, where there are many big cities, light up brightly at night. This is because when many people live in one area, the combined lights of all the buildings at night are so bright they show up as a dot.

Mount Vesuvius

Mount Vesuvius is a volcano near the city of Naples in southern Italy. It is famous for its eruption in AD79, which buried the towns of Pompeii and Herculaneum in around 30m (100ft) of ash, mud and stones. The towns remained buried until the 18th century when they were rediscovered.

Vesuvius is monitored very carefully today, as it is close to the city of Naples and more than two million people live nearby. It has had over 50 minor eruptions since the one in AD79.

This satellite image of Europe was taken at night, but the land and water have been falsely-shaded, so you can see their outlines clearly. Each blue dot represents a highly populated area that is lit up.

Internet links

For links to websites where you can explore the Rhine and other rivers of Europe, go to **www.usborne-quicklinks.com**

This area of the Alps is in Switzerland. Over 70% of Switzerland is mountainous.

The Rhine River

The Rhine River carries more traffic than any other river in the world. It is 1,320km (820 miles) long and winds through the west of Europe, flowing from the Alps in Switzerland, along the Swiss-Austrian border, through Germany and France to the Netherlands. Many cities lie along its banks, including Strasbourg, in France, and Cologne, in Germany.

This is a section of the Rhine River running through west Germany. The river is black, vegetation is blue and buildings are brown. The patchwork of rectangles to the east of the river is farmland.

Norwegian fjords

Norway's dramatic coastline is a mixture of steep mountains and long, thin inlets of water, called fjords. The fjords were formed by glaciers. When glacier ice builds up at the top of a mountain, it becomes heavy and starts to slide down the slopes, carving out a deep channel in the rock. When the glacier melts, the water fills the channel, making a fjord.

The satellite image below shows an area of Norway's coastline. The long, thin blue strips are inlets of water, called fjords.

Eastern Europe stretches as far as the Ural Mountains, which separate European Russia from Asian Russia. Northern Europe is made up of Iceland and the Scandinavian countries, including Norway and Sweden.

Onion-shaped domes

Early Russian churches have an easily recognizable style, with high walls, very few doors and windows, and steeply-sloped roofs topped with onion-shaped domes. This style became popular during the 11th century. Many of these early churches were built from wood, as it was a building material widely available from Russia's dense forests.

This is the Church of the Intercession on Kizhi Island in northern Russia. It was built almost entirely from wood in 1764.

This is a Viking helmet. It was discovered in a grave in Uppland, Sweden.

Viking lands

During the 9th to the 11th centuries, the Vikings, a group of master ship builders and sea traders from Scandinavia, dominated northern Europe. Viking heritage can still be seen today. The Vikings carved stories and pictures into large stones, called rune stones. Many of these stones have survived and give clues to how they lived. The Viking Ship Museum in Oslo, Norway, has three well-preserved Viking ships, and in Sweden, a Viking festival is held each year in a reconstructed Viking village.

In this dramatic image of Budapest you can see the Chain Bridge, which links Buda and Pest across the Danube River.

Internet links

For a link to a website where you can print out a Viking map game, go to **www.usborne-quicklinks.com**

Danube River

The Danube River flows from the west to the east of Europe, through many major cities, including Bratislava, the capital of Slovakia, and Budapest, the capital of Hungary. The river splits Budapest into two parts, Buda and Pest. The Royal Palace is in Buda, on the west bank, while Hungary's parliament building is in Pest, on the east bank.

Atlantic puffins

One type of bird common throughout northern Europe is the Atlantic puffin. Atlantic puffins are sea birds that live in the cold waters around the coasts of the North Atlantic Ocean.

Atlantic puffins are very skilled at diving underwater to catch fish to eat. They only come ashore once a year to nest on rocky cliff tops and grassy islands. Iceland has the largest puffin population in the world at around nine million.

These are Atlantic puffins. They are about 18cm (10in) tall and have yellow, orange and blue beaks, which is why they are also known as sea parrots.

The west of Europe stretches as far as Portugal on the Atlantic coast, while southern Europe reaches down to the many small islands in the Mediterranean Sea, where the climate is famously sunny, warm and dry.

Sights of London

There are many famous sights in London, from the huge clock tower of Big Ben, to Buckingham Palace, the official residency of the Queen.

One of the city's most recent additions is the London Eye, the world's largest Ferris wheel, which was constructed to mark the millennium. The top of the wheel is 135m (443ft) high, giving an impressive view of the city.

The London Eye sits on the south bank of the River Thames. Big Ben sits on the opposite bank.

Internet links

For a link to a website where you can send virtual postcards of famous landmarks in Europe, go to **www.usborne-quicklinks.com**

Eiffel Tower

The Eiffel Tower in Paris, France, was opened in 1889, and has since had over 200 million visitors. It was built for an international exhibition celebrating the scientific and engineering achievements of the time. The iron structure is around 300m (980ft) tall and has three levels with many shops and restaurants.

There are over 350 electric lamps fitted to the outside of the Eiffel Tower, lighting it up dramatically at night.

The Leaning Tower

One of Italy's most famous sights is the Leaning Tower of Pisa. The 55m (180ft) tall bell tower is part of Pisa Cathedral. Building work began on it in 1173, and the tower started to lean while it was being built. It leans because the ground beneath it is a mixture of sand and clay, which are easily compressed. The huge weight of the tower compressed the ground more in some areas than others, so the tower began to lean.

This marble statue of a discus thrower is a copy of a bronze statue from 5th-century Greece. The statue, housed in the National Museum in Rome, Italy, is a symbol of the Olympic games.

Home of the Olympics

Athletes from all over the world compete in the Olympic games every four years. The first Olympic games were held in celebration of the Greek God Zeus in Olympia, Greece, in 776BC. Today, some of the foundations, steps and pillars of the original stadium, which seated around 30,000 spectators, remain. The start and finish lines of the running track, and the judges' seats, have also survived.

Mikkeli
Hameenlinna
Paijanne Lake
Pihlaja Lake
20°E
Turku
Lahtio
FINLAND
Kouvola
Saimaa Lake
Aland Islands
Espoo
Lappeenranta
Helsinki
Kotka
Vyborg
Zelenogorsk
Lake Ladoga
Lake Onega
Konosha

Baltic Sea
Gulf of Finland
St. Petersburg
Tallinn
Hiiumaa
Kohtla-Jarve
Pushkin
Volkhov
Tikhvin
White Lake
Haapsalu
Narva
Kingisepp
Gatchina
ESTONIA
Kuressaare
Saaremaa
Parnu
Kirishi
Vologda
Cherepovets
Konosha

2
Ventspils
Gulf of Riga
Tartu
Lake Peipus
Novgorod
Borovichi
Rybinsk Reservoir
Vologda

Jurmala
Cesis
Voru
Lake Pskov
Pskov
Lake Ilmen
Valdai Hills
Vyshniy Volochek
Rybinsk
Kostroma
Jelgava
Riga
Aluksne
North
343m (1,125ft)
Yaroslavl
Kineshma
Volga
Siauliai
LATVIA
Jekabpils
Ludza
Opochka
Velikiye Luki
European
Ivanovo
Gorki Reservoir
Semer
55°N
Panevezys
Daugavpils
Tver
Sergiyev Posad
Nizhni
LITHUANIA
Western Dvina
Navapolatsk
Polatsk
Rzhev
Zelenograd
Vladimir
Oka
Novgo
Kaunas
Plain
Marijampole
Vitsyebsk
Podolsk
Moscow
Murom
Alytus
Vilnius
Maladzyechna
Orsha
Dnieper
Smolensk
Obninsk
Kolomna
Arzam
Hrodna
Lida
Barysaw
Kaluga
Serpukhov
Ryazan
Minsk
Zhodzina
Roslavl
Oka
Tula
3
Baranavichy
BELARUS
Mahilyow
293m (961ft)
Sarans
Slutsk
Babruysk
Bryansk
Michurinsk
Kamenka
Salihorsk
Zhlobin
Orel
Yelets
Lipetsk
Tambov
Penza
Pinsk
Pripet Marshes
Svyetlahorsk
Homyel
Klintsy
Desna
Central
Pripet
Mazyr
Rechytsa
Russian
Lutsk
Chernihiv
Kursk
Voronezh
Korosten
Staryy Oskol
Uplands
Shepetivka
Kievske Reservoir
50°
Zhytomyr
Kiev
Sumy
417m (1,368ft)
Dnieper
Khmelnytskyy
Bila Tserkva
Lubny
Kharkiv
Vinnytsya
Kremenchukske Reservoir
Poltava
Kamyanets-Podilskyy
Cherkasy
Kremenchuk
Slovyansk
Lysychansk
Kamys
Uman
UKRAINE
Kramatorsk
Volgograd
4
Botosani
Balti
Kirovohrad
Oleksandriya
Dniprodzerzhynsk
Dnipropetrovsk
Horlivka
Luhansk
Rabnita
Kryvyy Rih
Donets
Iasi
MOLDOVA
Yuzhnoukrayinsk
Zaporizhzhya
Donetsk
Chisinau
Nikopol
Tsimlyansk Reservoir
ROMANIA
Tighina
Tiraspol
Mykolayiv
Kakhovske Reservoir
Mariupol
Novocherkassk
Volgodonsk
Bilhorod Dnistrovskyy
Odesa
Kherson
Melitopol
Don
Rostov
Galati
Berdyansk
Braila
Black Sea
Sea of Azov
Tulcea
Mouths of the Danube
45°

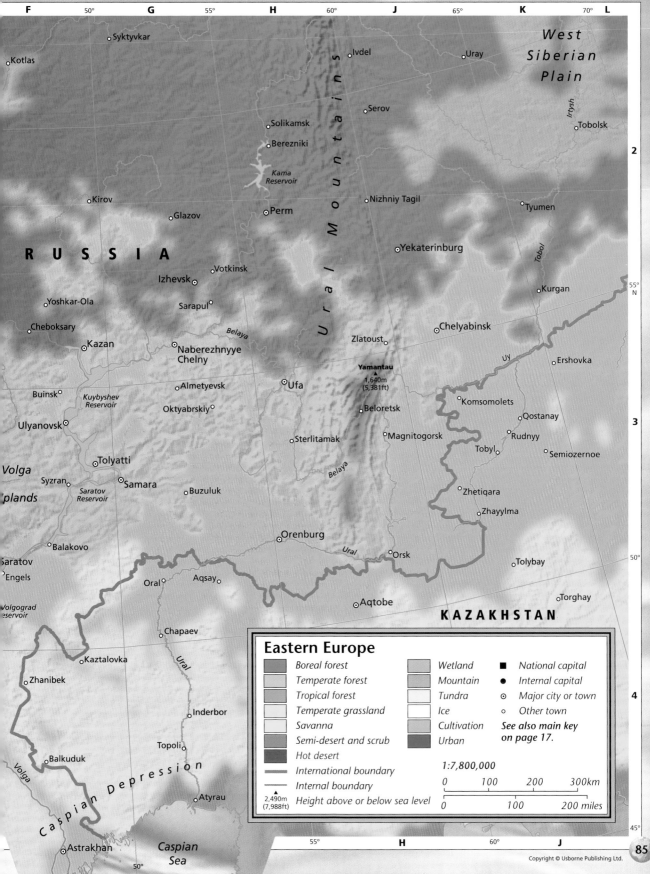

F 50° G 55° H 60° J 65° K 70° L

West Siberian Plain

Kotlas

Syktyvkar

Ivdel

Uray

2

Serov

Solikamsk

Tobolsk

Berezniki

Irtysh

Kama Reservoir

Kirov

Nizhniy Tagil

Tyumen

Glazov

Perm

Yekaterinburg

R U S S I A

Tobol

Izhevsk

Votkinsk

55° N

Yoshkar-Ola

Sarapul

Kurgan

U r a l   M o u n t a i n s

Cheboksary

Belaya

Zlatoust

Chelyabinsk

Kazan

Naberezhnyye Chelny

Uy

Ershovka

Buinsk

Kuybyshev Reservoir

Almetyevsk

Ufa

Yamantau
▲
1,640m
(5,381ft)

Komsomolets

Ulyanovsk

Oktyabrskiy

Beloretsk

Qostanay

Rudnyy

3

Tolyatti

Sterlitamak

Magnitogorsk

Tobyl

Semiozernoe

Volga

Syzran

Samara

Buzuluk

Belaya

Zhetiqara

plands

Saratov Reservoir

Zhayylma

Balakovo

Orenburg

Ural

Orsk

Tolybay

50°

Saratov

Engels

Oral

Aqsay

Volgograd
eservoir

Aqtobe

Torghay

K A Z A K H S T A N

Chapaev

4

Kaztalovka

Ural

Zhanibek

Inderbor

Topoli

Balkuduk

Caspian Depression

Volga

Atyrau

45°

55° H 60° J

Astrakhan

Caspian Sea

50°

Eastern Europe

Boreal forest
Temperate forest
Tropical forest
Temperate grassland
Savanna
Semi-desert and scrub
Hot desert
International boundary
Internal boundary
▲ 2,490m (7,988ft) Height above or below sea level

Wetland
Mountain
Tundra
Ice
Cultivation
Urban

■ National capital
● Internal capital
⊙ Major city or town
○ Other town

See also main key on page 17.

1:7,800,000

0   100   200   300km

0   100   200 miles

CENTRAL AND NORTHERN EUROPE—MAP

Barents Sea

Kola Peninsula

White Sea

RUSSIA

North Cape
Vadso
Kirkenes
Severomorsk
Murmansk
Utsjoki
Sevettijarvi
Kaamanen
Monchegorsk
▲1,191m
3,907ft) Apatity
Kandalaksha
Belomorsk
Lake Vyg
Lake Onega
Lake Seg
Petrozavodsk
Medvezhyegorsk
Lake Top
Lake Kuyto
Kostomuksha
Lake Pya
Lake Ladoga
Zelenogorsk
Vyborg
St. Petersburg
Pushkin
Gatchina
Kingisepp
Volkhov
Tikhvin
Kirishi
Borovichi
Novgorod
Lake Ilmen
Lake Peipus

Lapland

Lake Inari
Sodankyla
Lokan Reservoir
Kuusamo
Kuhmo
Kajaani
Lieksa
Pielis Lake
Oulu Lake
Rovaniemi
Tornio
Oulu
Raahe
Kokkola
Kuopio
Varkaus
Kiuruvesi
Hauki Lake
Pihlaja Lake
Saimaa Lake
Lappeenranta
Kouvola
Kotka
Narva

Hammerfest
Soroya
Alta
Tromso

Kebnekaise
▲2,114m
(6,935ft)
Narvik
Svolvaer
Vestfjorden
Lofoten
Vesterålen
Bodo
Moi
Rana

FINLAND

Kiruna
Stora Lule Lake
Horn Lake
Storavan Lake
Boden
Ume
Skelleftea
Umea
Gulf of Bothnia
Vaasa
Kurikka
Saarijarvi
Alavus
Jyvaskyla
Mikkeli
Puula Lake
Paljanne Lake
Nasi Lake
Tampere
Hameenlinna
Lahti
Helsinki
Espoo
Turku
Pori
Rauma
Aland Islands
Hiiumaa
Haapsalu
Tallinn
ESTONIA
Gulf of Finland
Kohtla-Jarve
Saarenmaa

Namsos
Steinkjer
Vikna
Trondheim
Oppdal
Stor Lake
Ostersund
Indals
Sundsvall
Hudiksvall
Gavle
Uppsala
Eskilstuna
Lake Malar
Stockholm
Sodertalje

Norwegian Sea

NORWAY

Galdhopiggen
▲2,469m
(8,100ft)
Froya
Hitra
Smola
Kristiansund
Alesund
Sula
Sotra
Bergen
Odda
Stavanger
Karmoy
Varhaug

Lillehammer
Glama
Honefoss
Oslo
Drammen
Fredrikstad
Larvik
Arendal

SWEDEN

Borlange
Dal
Klar
Karlstad
Orebro
Lake Vaner
Vingaker

Inset map — ICELAND:

Langanes
Seydhisfjordhur
Siglufjordhur
Isafjordhur
Faxafloi
Keflavik
Reykjavik
ICELAND
Vatnajokull
Hvannadalshnukur
▲2,119m
(6,952ft)
Same scale as main map
ATLANTIC OCEAN
Arctic Circle

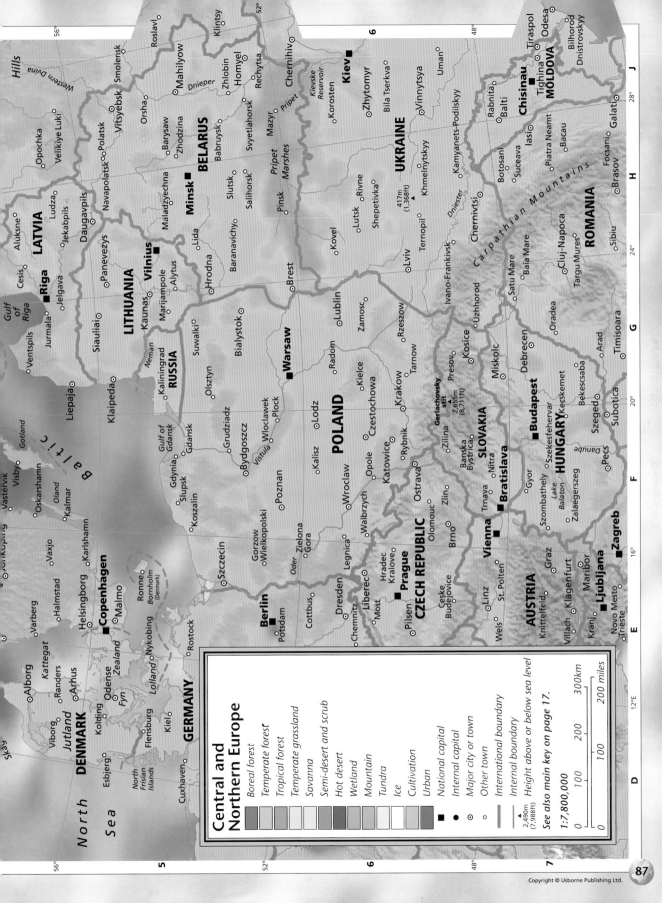

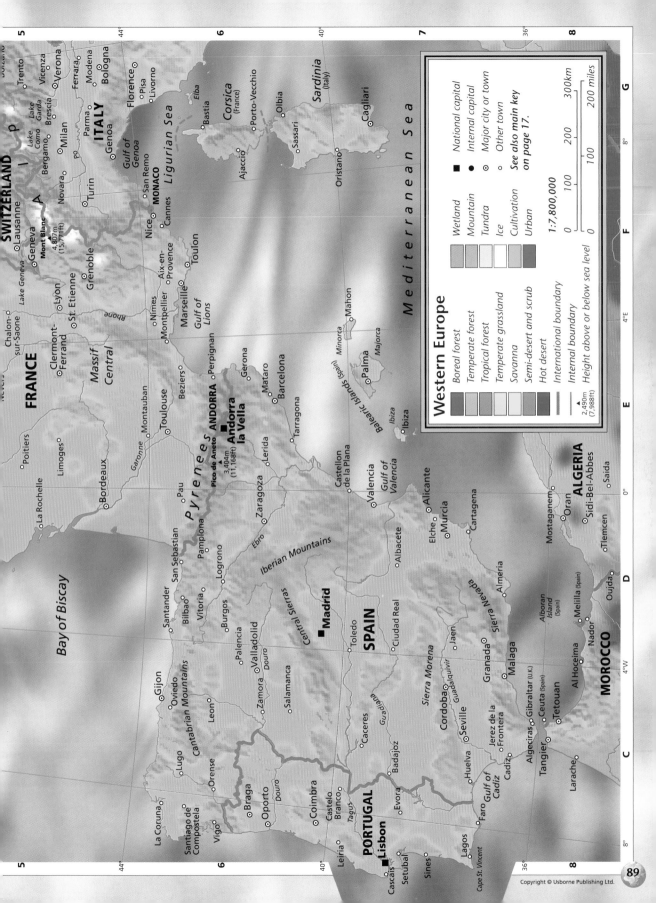

Southern Europe

	Boreal forest
	Temperate forest
	Tropical forest
	Temperate grassland
	Savanna
	Semi-desert and scrub
	Hot desert
	Wetland
	Mountain
	Tundra
	Ice
	Cultivation
	Urban
■	National capital
●	Internal capital
⊙	Major city or town
○	Other town
──	International boundary
──	Internal boundary
▲ 2,490m (7,988ft)	Height above or below sea level

See also main key on page 17.

1:7,800,000

0   100   200   300km

0   100   200 miles

Map labels:

A 0° B 4°E C 8° D 12° E 16°

Cherbourg, Le Havre, Caen, Rouen, Amiens, Charleroi, Namur, Koblenz, Frankfurt, Erfurt, Gera, Chemnitz, Dresden, Wroclaw, Walbrzy

BELGIUM, LUXEMBOURG, ■Luxembourg, Most, Liberec, Hradec Kralove, Karlovy Vary, Pilsen, ●Prague, CZECH REPUBLIC, Olomouc, ZI

Paris■, Evry, Reims, Metz, Saarbrucken, Mannheim, Wurzburg, Nuremberg, GERMANY, Karlsruhe, Regensburg, Ingolstadt, Ceske Budejovice, Brno

Le Mans, Troyes, Nancy, Stuttgart, Augsburg, Linz, St. Polten, Vienna■, Brno

Angers, Tours, Orleans, Dijon, Strasbourg, Freiburg, Ulm, Munich, Wels, Bratisla■

Poitiers, Nevers, Besancon, Basel, Winterthur, Kempten, Salzburg, Trn

FRANCE, Chalon-sur-Saone, Biel, Bern■, Lucerne, Zurich, Innsbruck, Knittelfeld, Szombathe

Limoges, Geneva, Lausanne, SWITZERLAND, ■Vaduz, LIECHTENSTEIN, Grossglockner 3,798m (12,461ft), AUSTRIA, Graz, Zalaegers, Bala

Clermont-Ferrand, Lake Geneva, Mont Blanc 4,807m (15,771ft), Bolzano, Villach, Klagenfurt, Maribor

St. Etienne, Grenoble, Novara, Trento, Bergamo, Lake Como, Lake Garda, Vicenza, Kranj, Novo Mesto, SLOVENIA, ■Ljubljana, ■Zagreb, CROATI

Massif Central, Lyon, Turin, Milan, Brescia, Verona, Venice, Trieste, Rijeka, Karlovac, Slavo

Garonne, Rhone, Po, Parma, Modena, Ferrara, Bologna, Pula, Banja Luka, BOSNIA

Montauban, Toulouse, Nimes, Genoa, Gulf of Genoa, Ravenna, Rimini, ITALY, Zadar, AND HERZEGOVI, Ze

Montpellier, Aix-en-Provence, MONACO, Nice, San Remo, SAN MARINO, Ancona, Split, Mo

Beziers, ■Andorra la Vella, Gulf of Lions, Marseille, Cannes, Pisa, Livorno, Florence, Perugia, Pescara, Adriatic Sea

Toulon, Ligurian Sea, Bastia, Elba, Terni, Apennines

Corsica (France), Ajaccio, Porto-Vecchio, VATICAN CITY, ■Rome, Foggia, Bari

Olbia, Sassari, Naples, Pompeii, Salerno, Taranto

Oristano, Sardinia (Italy), Tyrrhenian Sea, Cosenza, Catanzar

Cagliari, Mediterranean Sea, Lipari Islands

Annaba, Menzel Bourguiba, Bizerte, Carthage, ■Tunis, Trapani, Palermo, Messina, Sicily, Mount Etna 3,323m (10,902ft), Catania

Guelma, Agrigento, Syracuse

Souk Ahras, Nabeul, Pantelleria (Italy), Ragusa, MALTA, ■Valletta

TUNISIA, Sousse, Pelagian Islands (Italy)

Tebessa, Kairouan, Monastir

Kasserine, El Jem, Biskra

B 4°E C 8° D 12° E 16°

Kielce
Czestochowa
owice
Zamosc
Lutsk
Rivne
Zhytomyr
Kiev
Lubny
Poltava
Slovyansk

POLAND
ybnik
Krakow
Tarnow
Rzeszow
Vistula
Lviv
Shepetivka
Bila Tserkva
Cherkasy
Kremenchukske
Reservoir
Kremenchuk
Kramatorsk
1
trava

Zilina
Gerlachovsky
stit
▲ 2,655m
(8,711ft)
Presov
Ternopil
417m
(1,368ft)
Khmelnytskyy
Vinnytsya
UKRAINE
Dniprodzerzhynsk
Oleksandriya
Dnipropetrovsk
48°
N

Banska
Bystrica
Kosice
Uzhhorod
Ivano-Frankivsk
Dniester
Kamyanets-
Podilskyy
Uman
Kirovohrad
Dnieper
Zaporizhzhya

OVAKIA
Miskolc
Chernivtsi
Chernivtsi
Rabnita
Kryvyy Rih
Nikopol
Kakhovske
Reservoir
Berdyansk

Satu Mare
Botosani
Balti
Yuzhnoukrayinsk
Mykolayiv
Melitopol
2

Budapest
Debrecen
Baia Mare
Suceava
Iasi
MOLDOVA
Kherson
*Sea of
Azov*

kesfehervar
Oradea
Cluj-Napoca
Piatra Neamt
Tighina
Chisinau
Tiraspol
Odesa
Dzhankoy
Kerch

UNGARY
skemet
Bekescsaba
Arad
Targu Mures
Bacau
Bilhorod-
Dnistrovskyy
Crimea
Feodosiya

Szeged
ROMANIA
Focsani
Galati
Yevpatoriya
Simferopol

Subotica
Timisoara
Sibiu
Mount
Moldoveanu
2,544m
(8,346ft)
▲
Brasov
Braila
Tulcea
Sevastopol
44°

Osijek
Novi Sad
Arad
Transylvanian Alps
Ramnicu Valcea
Buzau
*Mouths of
the Danube*

uzla
Belgrade
Pitesti
Ploiesti
Bucharest
Constanta
Black Sea

**SERBIA AND
MONTENEGRO**
Drobeta-Turnu Severin
Craiova
Danube
Ruse
Dobrich

arajevo
Kragujevac
Pleven
Varna
3

Kraljevo
Nis
Vratsa
Shumen

Niksic
Leskovac
Balkan Mountains
BULGARIA
Sliven
Burgas

ovnik
Vranje
Pristina
Sofia
Stara Zagora
Zonguldak
Karabuk

gorica
Tetovo
Kumanovo
Plovdiv
Edirne
Bosporus
Adapazari
Corum

Shkoder
Skopje
Blagoevgrad
Istanbul
Ankara
Kirikkale

Durres
Tirana
Prilep
MACEDONIA
Serres
Kavala
Tekirdag
*Sea of
Marmara*
Eskisehir
40°

Elbasan
Bitola
Thessaloniki
Thasos
Bursa

ALBANIA
Korce
Mount Olympus
2,917m
(9,570ft)
▲
Canakkale
Balikesir
Kutahya
Lake Tuz

Vlore
Pindus Mountains
Limnos
TURKEY
Aksaray

Corfu
Ioannina
Larisa
*Aegean
Sea*
Lesvos
Akhisar
Usak
4

Corfu
Volos
Euboea
Skyros
Manisa
Konya

GREECE
Lamia
Chios
Izmir
Odemis
*Beysehir
Lake*

Kefallonia
Chalkida
Ephesus
Denizli
Karaman

Preveza
Patra
Peiraias
Athens
Aydin
Antalya
Taurus Mountains

Pyrgos
Alanya

nian Sea
Kalamata
Cyclades
*Gulf of
Antalya*

Kythira
Rhodes
Kyrenia

Rhodes
Nicosia

Chania
Crete
Karpathos
CYPRUS
Larnaca

Irakleio
Paphos
Limassol

Ierapetra

AFRICA

Africa is the second-biggest continent in the world, and has 53 countries. These range from the vast, dry Sudan, to small, tropical islands such as the Seychelles. More than a quarter of Africa's countries are landlocked, with no access to the sea except through other countries.

Here is a group of Masai people from East Africa, silhouetted against a sunset over the flat grasslands of Africa.

Algiers
Tunis
Rabat
Madeira
(Portugal)
MOROCCO
TUNISIA
Tripoli
Canary Islands
(Spain)
Laayoune
ALGERIA
LIBYA
Tropic of Cancer
WESTERN
SAHARA
(Morocco)
MAURITANIA
Nouakchott
MALI
NIGER
Niger
CHAD
CAPE VERDE
Praia
Dakar
SENEGAL
Niamey
Ndjame
THE GAMBIA
Banjul
Bamako
Ouagadougou
Bissau
GUINEA-BISSAU
GUINEA
BURKINA FASO
NIGERIA
Conakry
BENIN
Abuja
Freetown
IVORY
COAST
TOGO
CENT
AFRI
REPU
SIERRA LEONE
GHANA
Porto-Novo
Monrovia
Yamoussoukro
Lome
CAMEROON
Bangui
LIBERIA
Accra
Malabo
Yaounde
EQUATORIAL
GUINEA
CO
Equator
Libreville
CONGO
SAO TOME
AND PRINCIPE
GABON
Brazzaville
Kinshas
ATLANTIC
Luanda
OCEAN
ANGOLA
NAMIBIA
Tropic of Capricorn
Windhoek
Oran
Cape Town

The shading on this map is there to help you see clearly the different countries that make up the continent.

EGYPT

Cairo

Tropic of Cancer

Nile

Khartoum

SUDAN

ERITREA
Asmara

DJIBOUTI Djibouti

Addis Ababa

SOMALIA

ETHIOPIA

UGANDA
Kampala

NGO

KENYA

Kigali

Nairobi

EM.

RWANDA
BURUNDI
Bujumbura

Mogadishu

Equator

EP.)

Dodoma

Victoria

TANZANIA

Dar es Salaam

SEYCHELLES

MALAWI

Lilongwe

Moroni
COMOROS

INDIAN

AMBIA
Lusaka

OCEAN

ambezi

Harare
ZIMBABWE

MOZAMBIQUE

Antananarivo

TSWANA

MADAGASCAR

MAURITIUS
Port Louis

orone

Reunion
(France)

Tropic of Capricorn

Pretoria

Maputo

Mbabane
SWAZILAND
Lobamba

emfontein

Maseru

LESOTHO

UTH
RICA

Facts

Total land area 30,311,690 sq km (11,703,343 sq miles)
Total population 794 million
Biggest city Lagos, Nigeria
Biggest country Sudan *2,505,810 sq km (967,493 sq miles)*
Smallest country Seychelles *455 sq km (176 sq miles)*

Highest mountain Kilimanjaro, Tanzania *5,895m (19,340ft)*
Longest river Nile, running from Burundi to Egypt *6,671km (4,145 miles)*
Biggest lake Lake Victoria, between Tanzania, Kenya and Uganda *69,215 sq km (26,724 sq miles)*
Highest waterfall Tugela Falls, on the Tugela River, South Africa *610m (2,000ft)*
Biggest desert Sahara, North Africa *9,100,000 sq km (3,500,000 sq miles)*
Biggest island Madagascar *587,040 sq km (226,656 sq miles)*

Main mineral deposits Gold, copper, diamonds, iron ore, manganese, bauxite
Main fuel deposits Coal, uranium, natural gas

This greater flamingo is from the Transvaal National Park, South Africa.

Africa is home to the world's longest river, the Nile, and its largest desert, the Sahara. In southern Africa there are two more large deserts, the Kalahari and the Namib. Africa also has enormous rainforests in central areas, near the Equator.

A convoy of camels moves across the Sahara Desert in North Africa. The strange swirls of sand are formed by strong winds.

Desert weather

Temperatures in the Sahara Desert can rise as high as 55°C (131°F) during the day, but often fall below freezing point at night. Strong winds blow across the desert and whip up mini whirlwinds called dust devils. These suck up sand and hurl it high into the air.

This satellite image clearly shows the vast Sahara Desert in North Africa. It covers an area about the size of the U.S.A.

Moroccan mountain life

The Atlas Mountains dominate the country of Morocco, north of the Sahara Desert. High in the mountains are villages which are home to groups of African people called Berbers. Berbers have lived in Morocco for thousands of years and today still follow their traditional way of life, herding sheep and goats.

This image shows the curves and folds of the Atlas Mountains in Morocco. They were formed by earthquakes and other movements of the Earth.

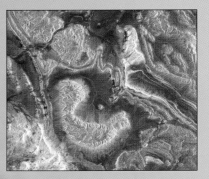

The dark blue water in the lower right of this satellite image is the Red Sea. The triangular piece of land jutting into it is part of Egypt.

River in the desert

The River Nile winds its way through eastern Africa, from Burundi all the way to the Mediterranean Sea. It is almost the only water source in this dry, arid part of Africa, so major cities, such as Cairo in Egypt, have grown up near it. The soil near the Nile's banks is fertile enough to farm on, especially near the coast where the river splits into many streams.

Wild forests

The large, dense rainforests of central Africa are home to more than half of Africa's wild animals, including chimpanzees, gorillas and elephants. Many of these animals have never come into contact with humans.

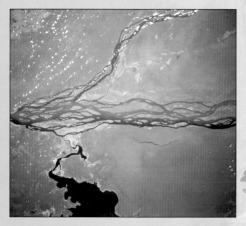

The dense rainforest of central Africa is pink in this satellite image. Running across the middle of the picture is the large Congo River. It splits into many smaller rivers, creating a huge swampy area.

This is the River Nile, running through Egypt. As the river reaches the sea, it splits into many streams that create an expanse of fertile, swampy land. This is the large green area at the top of the image.

One of Africa's most populous countries is Egypt, which has busy cities such as its capital, Cairo, as well as the remains of ancient civilizations. Africa also has many areas of natural beauty, such as the vast wildlife parks in the south and east of the continent.

Pyramids and the Sphinx

One of the ancient wonders of the world is found at Giza, in Egypt – the group of three Great Pyramids. These stone structures were built by the ancient Egyptians as tombs for their pharaohs, or kings. The biggest pyramid is about 140m (480ft) high, and probably took 20 years to build. You can see a picture of the pyramids on page 1 of this atlas.

In front of the pyramids stands the Great Sphinx, an enormous statue of a lion with a man's head. It was probably carved as a monument to a pharaoh, though no one is sure which one. Some historians believe there are secret rooms and tunnels underneath the Sphinx.

This is the Great Sphinx of Egypt. It was carved out of soft limestone which has crumbled over the years. Part of the Sphinx's nose is now missing.

Cape Town

At Africa's southern tip, in the country of South Africa, is the city of Cape Town. It is famous for its elegant buildings, sandy beaches and busy waterfront. The city is right next to Table Mountain, which gets its name from its distinctive flat top. Thick clouds often cover the mountain and are nicknamed the Table Cloth.

This is Cape Town, with Table Mountain behind.

A panther chameleon clings to a branch. It can wrap its tail around the branch too, for extra grip. Panther chameleons live only in Madagascar.

On safari

Wild animals such as lions, elephants, buffaloes and zebras live on the grasslands of eastern and southern Africa. The land is divided into many specially protected wildlife parks that tourists can visit on safari trips.

These parks are some of the last remaining places where cheetahs live. These big cats were once found all over Africa but are now endangered. Cheetahs are the world's fastest land animals, able to run at a speed of 115kph (70mph).

Wildlife island

Madagascar is a large island in the Indian Ocean, off Africa's southeastern coast. It has thick, steamy rainforests which are home to many animals not found anywhere else in the world. These include rare chameleons and over 50 species of monkey-like animals called lemurs.

Internet links

For links to websites where you can see the Sphinx, explore an Egyptian pyramid and go on a photo safari, go to **www.usborne-quicklinks.com**

A cheetah in Kenya, eastern Africa, hisses and spits fiercely to scare away enemies.

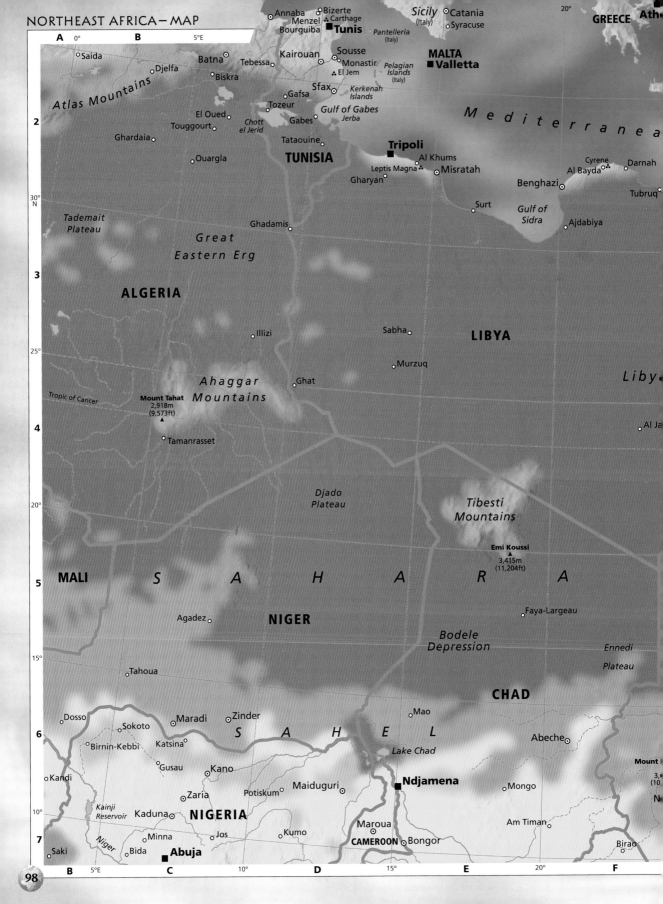

NORTHEAST AFRICA—MAP

A 0°   **B** 5°E

Saida

Djelfa

Batna   Tebessa

Biskra

Atlas Mountains

Ghardaia

El Oued   Touggourt

Chott el Jerid

Gafsa   Tozeur

Ouargla

2

Gabes

Tataouine

TUNISIA

Annaba   Bizerte
Menzel   Carthage
Bourguiba   **Tunis**

Kairouan

Sousse
Monastir
El Jem

Sfax

Kerkenah Islands

Gulf of Gabes

Jerba

Sicily (Italy)   Catania
Syracuse

Pantelleria (Italy)

Pelagian Islands (Italy)

**MALTA
Valletta**

GREECE   **Ath**

20°

M e d i t e r r a n e a

Tripoli

Al Khums

Leptis Magna   **Misratah**

Gharyan

Cyrene

Al Bayda   Darnah

Benghazi

Tubruq

30° N

ALGERIA

Tademait Plateau

Great
Eastern Erg

Ghadamis

Surt

Gulf of Sidra

Ajdabiya

3

Illizi

Sabha

LIBYA

Liby

Murzuq

4

Ahaggar
Mountains

Ghat

Tropic of Cancer

Mount Tahat
2,918m
(9,573ft)
▲

Tamanrasset

Al Ja

5

MALI

S   *A*   *H*   *A*   *R*   *A*

Djado
Plateau

*Tibesti
Mountains*

Emi Koussi
▲
3,415m
(11,204ft)

20°

Agadez

NIGER

Faya-Largeau

*Bodele
Depression*

*Ennedi
Plateau*

15°

Tahoua

CHAD

Dosso

Sokoto

Maradi   Zinder

S   *A*   *H*   *E*   *L*

Mao

Abeche

Mount

3,
(10,

6

Birnin-Kebbi

Katsina

Gusau

Kano

Lake Chad

Kandi

Zaria

Potiskum

Maiduguri

Ndjamena

Mongo

Am Timan

*Kainji
Reservoir*

Kaduna

NIGERIA

Kumo

Maroua

CAMEROON   Bongor

Birao

7

Saki

Minna

Bida

Abuja

Jos

Niger

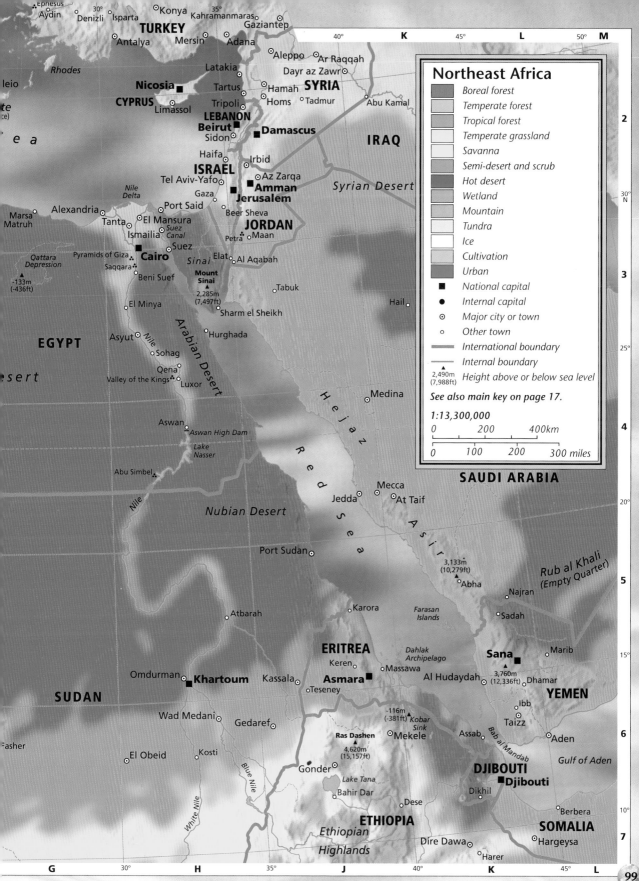

Epnesus
Aydin · 30°· Isparta · Konya · Kahramanmaras · 35°
Denizli · TURKEY · Gaziantep
Antalya · Mersin · Adana · 40° · K · 45° · L · 50° · M

Rhodes · Latakia · Aleppo · Ar Raqqah
Dayr az Zawr
Nicosia · Tartus · Hamah · SYRIA · Abu Kamal · 2
CYPRUS · Limassol · Tripoli · Homs · Tadmur
LEBANON · Beirut · Damascus · IRAQ
Sidon
Haifa · Irbid
ISRAEL · Az Zarqa · Syrian Desert · 30°
Tel Aviv-Yafo · Amman · N
Nile · Gaza · Jerusalem
Delta · Beer Sheva · JORDAN
Alexandria · Port Said · Maan
Marsa · Tanta · El Mansura · Petra
Matruh · Ismailia · Suez · Beer Sheva
Canal · Hail
Pyramids of Giza · Cairo · Sinai · Elat
Qattara · Saqqara · Suez · Al Aqabah · 3
Depression · Beni Suef · Mount
-133m · Sinai · Tabuk
(-436ft) · 2,285m
El Minya · (7,497ft)
Sharm el Sheikh · 25°
EGYPT · Asyut · Hurghada
Nile · Sohag
Qena · Medina
Valley of the Kings · Luxor
sert · Aswan
Aswan High Dam
Lake · 4
Nasser
SAUDI ARABIA
Abu Simbel · 1:13,300,000
Nile · Nubian Desert · Jedda · Mecca
At Taif · 20°
Port Sudan
SUDAN · 3,133m
(10,279ft)
Atbarah · Abha · 5
Karora · Farasan · Sadah
Islands · Najran
Dahlak
ERITREA · Archipelago · Sana · Marib
Omdurman · Keren · 3,760m · 15°
Khartoum · Kassala · Asmara · Massawa · (12,336ft) · Dhamar
Wad Medani · Teseney · Al Hudaydah · YEMEN
SUDAN · -116m · Ibb
Gedaref · (-381ft) Kobar · Taizz
El Fasher · Ras Dashen · Sink · Assab · Aden · 6
El Obeid · Kosti · 4,620m · Mekele
(15,157ft) · Gulf of Aden
Gonder · DJIBOUTI
Blue Nile · Lake Tana · Dikhil · Djibouti
White Nile · Bahir Dar · Dese · Berbera · 10°
ETHIOPIA · 7
Ethiopian · Dire Dawa · SOMALIA
Highlands · Harer · Hargeysa

G · 30° · H · 35° · J · 40° · K · 45° · L

Northeast Africa

Boreal forest
Temperate forest
Tropical forest
Temperate grassland
Savanna
Semi-desert and scrub
Hot desert
Wetland
Mountain
Tundra
Ice
Cultivation
Urban

■ National capital
● Internal capital
⊙ Major city or town
○ Other town

International boundary
Internal boundary

2,490m
(7,988ft) · Height above or below sea level

See also main key on page 17.

1:13,300,000

0 · 200 · 400km
0 · 100 · 200 · 300 miles

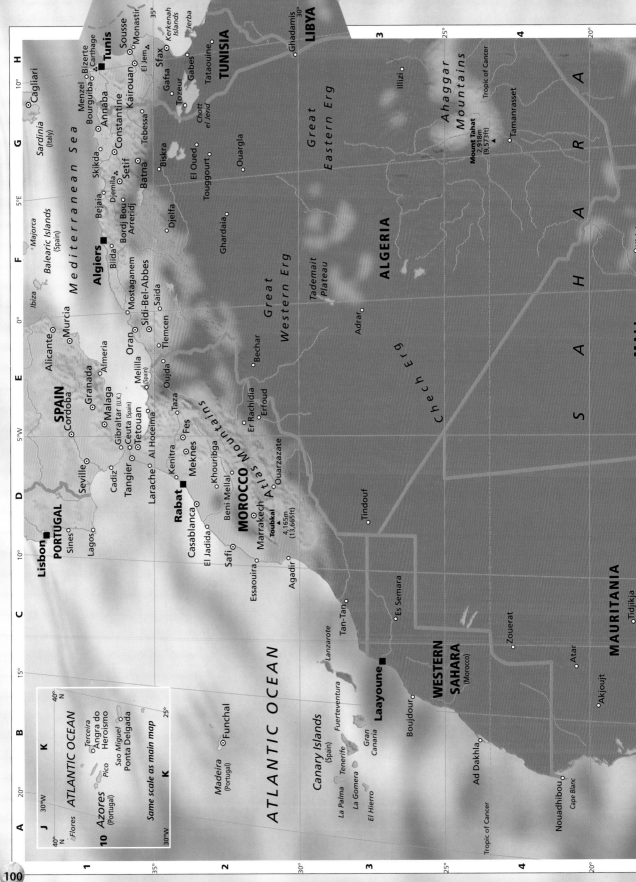

A | B | C | D | E | F | G | H

J
10

Flores
Azores
(Portugal)

40°
N

ATLANTIC OCEAN

Terceira
Angra do
Heroísmo
Pico
Sao Miguel
Ponta Delgada

Same scale as main map

40°
N

25°

30°W

K

K

Madeira
(Portugal)

Funchal

ATLANTIC OCEAN

Canary Islands
(Spain)

Lanzarote
Fuerteventura
Gran
Canaria
Tenerife
La Palma
La Gomera
El Hierro

Cagliari

Sardinia
(Italy)

Mediterranean Sea

Majorca
Balearic Islands
(Spain)

Ibiza

SPAIN

Cordoba
Granada
Seville
Malaga
Almeria
Gibraltar (U.K.)
Cadiz
Ceuta (Spain)
Tangier
Tetouan
Larache
Al Hoceima
Melilla
(Spain)
Oran
Sidi-Bel-Abbes
Tlemcen
Oujda
Taza
Fes
Kenitra
Meknes

Alicante
Murcia

PORTUGAL
Lisbon
Sines
Lagos

Rabat
Casablanca
El Jadida
Safi
Essaouira
Agadir
Beni Mellal
Khouribga
Marrakech
Toubkal
4,165m
(13,665ft)
Ouarzazate

MOROCCO

Atlas Mountains

Er Rachidia
Erfoud

Bechar

Menzel
Bourguiba
Bizerte
Annaba
Constantine
Skikda
Bejaia
Djemila
Setif
Batna
Tebessa
Biskra
El Oued
Touggourt
Ouargla
Ghardaia
Djelfa
Saida
Mostaganem
Blida
Algiers
Bordj Bou
Arreridj

Tunis
Carthage
Sousse
Monastir
Kairouan
El Jem
Sfax
Gafsa
Tozeur
Chott
el Jerid
Gabes
Tataouine
Kerkenah
Islands
Jerba

35°

TUNISIA

Ghadamis

LIBYA

30°

Great
Eastern Erg

Illizi

Ahaggar
Mountains

Mount Tahat
2,918m
(9,573ft)

Tamanrasset

Tropic of Cancer

ALGERIA

Great
Western Erg

Tademait
Plateau

Adrar

Chech Erg

S A H A R A

MALI

Tindouf

Es Semara

WESTERN
SAHARA
(Morocco)

Laayoune

Boujdour

Tan-Tan

ATLANTIC OCEAN

Zouerat

Atar

Akjoujt

Ad Dakhla

Nouadhibou
Cape Blanc

Tropic of Cancer

MAURITANIA

Tidjikja

30°W
20°
30°W

10°
5°W
0°
5°E
10°

25°
20°

1

35°

2

30°

3

25°

4

20°

Northwest Africa

Boreal forest
Temperate forest
Tropical forest
Temperate grassland
Savanna
Semi-desert and scrub
Hot desert

International boundary
Internal boundary

▲ 2,490m
(7,988ft)   Height above or below sea level

Wetland
Mountain
Tundra
Ice
Cultivation
Urban

1:13,300,000

■ National capital
● Internal capital
◉ Major city or town
○ Other town

*See also main key
on page 17.*

0   100   200   300 miles
0   200   400km

NIGER

Maradi
Tahoua
Katsina
Sokoto
Gusau
Birnin-Kebbi
Zaria
Kaduna
Minna
Bida
Abuja
Dosso
Ilorin
NIGERIA
Ogbomoso
Ibadan
Owo
Enugu
Onitsha
Warri
Benin City
Port Harcourt
Niger Delta
Abeokuta
Lagos
Porto-Novo
Cotonou
Saki
Kainji
Reservoir

Tombouctou
(Timbuktu)
Gao
Goundam
Mopti
Dori
Ouahigouya
Ouagadougou
BURKINA FASO
Fada-
Ngourma
Tenkodogo
Bawku
Niamey
Tillaberi
Kandi
Parakou
Natitingou
Djougou
BENIN
Abomey
TOGO
Sokode
Lome
Cotonou
Bight of Benin
Gulf of Guinea

Dosso
Tougan
Koudougou
Bobo Dioulasso
Banfora
Wa
Tamale
Damongo
Wenchi
GHANA
Lake Volta
Koforidua
Accra
Cape Coast
Sekondi-Takoradi
Tarkwa
Cape Three Points

Nema
Ayoun el
Atrous
Nioro du Sahel
Niono
Segou
San
Koutiala
Sikasso
Bougouni
Bamako
Odienne
Katiola
Bondoukou
Bouna
Korhogo
Bouake
IVORY COAST
Yamoussoukro
Adzope
Divo
Abidjan
Kumasi
Gagnoa
San Pedro
Cape Palmas

St. Louis
Louga
Thies
Dara
Dakar
Kaolack
SENEGAL
Tambacounda
Kolda
Kayes
Kita
Kedougou
Bignona
Ziguinchor
GUINEA-BISSAU
Bissau
Boke
Kindia
Conakry
GUINEA
Labe
Siguiri
Kankan
Gueckedou
Makeni
Sefadu
Bo
Kenema
Freetown
SIERRA LEONE
Zorzor
Tubmanburg
Monrovia
LIBERIA
Harper
Daloa
Man
Nzerekore
▲ 1,752m
(5,748ft)
Bissagos
Archipelago

Kaedi
Selibabi
Rosso

ATLANTIC OCEAN

Inset map

L 25°W **M**
Santo
Antao
ATLANTIC OCEAN
Sao Nicolau
Mindelo
Sal
Boa
Vista
11
CAPE VERDE
Sao Tiago
Maio
Praia
Fogo
15°
N
12
15°
N

Same scale as main map

**SAO TOME
AND PRINCIPE**
Principe
■ **Sao Tome**
Equator

5°E
0°
Gao

A 10°E · B · C 20° · D 25° · E

○Mao

Lake Chad

■ **Ndjamena**

Mount Marra ▲
3,088m
(10,131ft)

El Fasher

1

○Kano

○Maiduguri

○Potiskum

○Mongo

○Nyala

NIGERIA

CHAD

○Maroua

SUDAN

○Bongor

○Am Timan

10°

○Jos

○Kumo

○Garoua

○Lai

○Birao

2

○Makurdi

Lagdo
Reservoir

○Doba

Sarh○

○Ndele

○Ouadda

○Wau

○Moundou

○Ngaoundere

CENTRAL AFRICAN
REPUBLIC

○Bria

○Djema

○Bamenda

○Bossangoa

Foumban○

○Bozoum

○Bossembele

○Obo

CAMEROON

○Bouar

5°
N

○Bafoussam

○Calabar

○Nkongsamba

○Bangassou

○Kumba

○Bertoua

○Berberati

Uele

▲ Cameroon Mountain
4,095m
(13,435ft)

○Douala

■ **Bangui**

3

■ **Malabo**

■ **Yaounde**

○Gemena

○Buta

○Isiro

Bioco
(Equatorial
Guinea)

○Ebolowa

Congo

○Bata

○Oyem

Ubangi

Margherita
5,
(16,7

EQUATORIAL
GUINEA

○Ouesso

○Kisangani

Butembo

○Makokou

Mbandaka○

Lake
Edward

0°
Equator

■ **Libreville**

4,507m
(14,787ft)▲

Cape
Lopez

GABON

○Owando

Congo

○Goma
Lake Kivu

○Lambarene

○Lastoursville

CONGO

CONGO
(DEMOCRATIC
REPUBLIC)

RWAN

Port-
Gentil

○Moanda

○Franceville

Lake
Mai-Ndombe

Bukavu○ But

4

○Tchibanga

○Djambala

○Kindu

Bujumbura

○Mossendjo

○Bandundu

BURUN

○Sibiti

Congo

Kasai

Kigon

○Loubomo

■ **Brazzaville**

○Ilebo

5°
S

Pointe-Noire○

○Madingou

■ **Kinshasa**

○Kalemie

○Kinkala

○Kikwit

○Kananga

Lak
Tanganyik

CABINDA
(Angola)

○Kabinda

○Tshikapa

⊙Mbuji-Mayi

Pv

○Mwene-Ditu

○Kamina

○Mitwaba

○Marimba

○Kilwa

Lak
My

○Kamina

Sampwe○

○Kawambwa

■ **Luanda**

○Ndalatando

Cuango

○Saurimo

○Kafakumba

Bangw

Cape Ledo

○Dondo

○Malanje

○Kolwezi

○Mansa

5

ATLANTIC

○Dilolo

○Mutshatsha

○Likasi

○Lubumbas

○Kipushi

OCEAN

Cuanza

ANGOLA

○Quirima

○Luacano

Kasai

○Mwinilunga

○Solwezi

○Mufulira

○Kabu

6

2,620m
(8,596ft)▲

○Luena

○Lumbala

Zambezi

Chingola○

○Kitwe

○Ndo

○Benguela

Bie
Plateau

○Kuito

○Munhango

Kaquengue

○Chavuma

ZAMBIA

○Luanshya

○Huambo

A 10°E · B 15° · C 20° · D · E

Mk

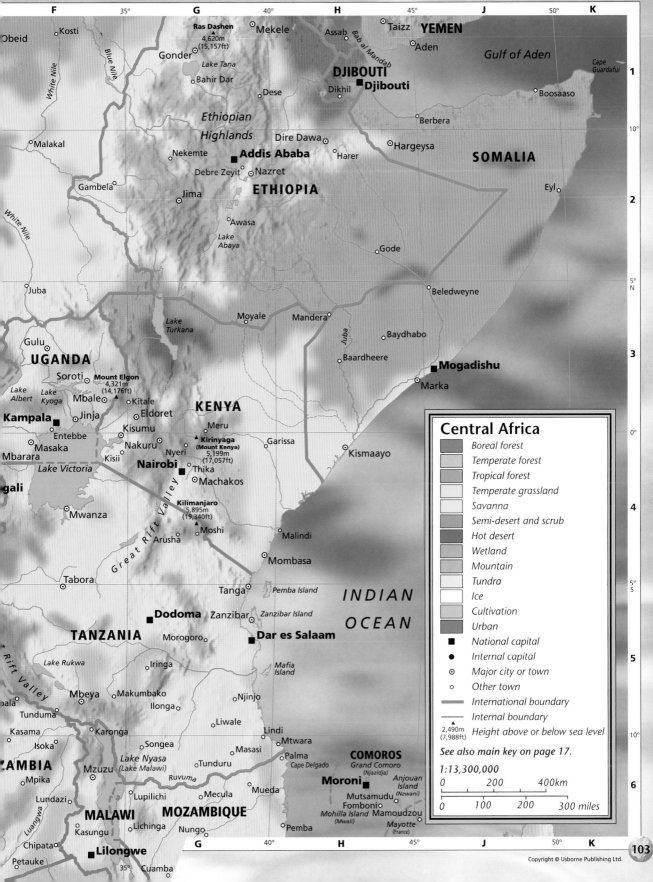

F · 35° · G · 40° · H · 45° · J · 50° · K

Obeid · Kosti

Ras Dashen
4,620m
(15,157ft) · Mekele

Gonder · Lake Tana

Bahir Dar · Dese

Taizz · **YEMEN**

Assab · Bab al Mandab · Aden

DJIBOUTI

Gulf of Aden

Cape
Guardafui

Dikhil · **Djibouti**

Boosaaso

1

*Ethiopian
Highlands*

Malakal

Dire Dawa · Berbera · 10°

Nekemte · **Addis Ababa** · Harer · Hargeysa

Debre Zeyit · **Nazret** · **SOMALIA**

Gambela · Jima · **ETHIOPIA**

White Nile

Eyl

2

Awasa

*Lake
Abaya*

Gode

Juba · 5°N

Beledweyne

Moyale · Mandera

Gulu · *Lake
Turkana*

Baydhabo

3

UGANDA · Soroti · Mount Elgon
4,321m
(14,176ft) · Baardheere

Juba

Mogadishu

Lake
Albert · Lake
Kyoga · Mbale · Kitale · Eldoret · **KENYA**

Marka

Kisumu · Meru

Kampala · Entebbe · Nakuru · Kirinyaga
(Mount Kenya)
5,199m
(17,057ft) · Garissa · 0°

Masaka · Kisii · Nyeri

Mbarara · **Nairobi** · Thika · Kismaayo

Lake Victoria · Machakos

gali · Kilimanjaro
5,895m
(19,340ft) · Moshi

Mwanza · Arusha

4

Malindi

Tabora · Mombasa · 5°S

Tanga · *Pemba Island* · **INDIAN**

Dodoma · Zanzibar · *Zanzibar Island* · **OCEAN**

TANZANIA · Morogoro · **Dar es Salaam**

Lake Rukwa · Iringa · *Mafia
Island*

5

Rift Valley · Mbeya · Makumbako · Ilonga · Njinjo

Kasama · Tunduma · Karonga · Liwale

Isoka · Songea · Lindi

ZAMBIA · Mzuzu · *Lake Nyasa
(Lake Malawi)* · Masasi · Mtwara

Mpika · Lichinga · Tunduru · Palma · *Cape Delgado*

COMOROS
Grand Comoro
(Njazidja)

Lundazi · Lupilichi · Mecula · Mueda

Anjouan
Island
(Nzwani)

Fomboni

Moroni · Mutsamudu

Mamoudzou · 6

Chipata · **MALAWI** · **MOZAMBIQUE** · Nungo · Mohilla Island
(Mwali)

Mayotte
(France)

Kasungu · Lichinga · Pemba

Petauke · **Lilongwe** · Cuamba

G · 40° · H · 45° · J · 50° · K

Central Africa

- Boreal forest
- Temperate forest
- Tropical forest
- Temperate grassland
- Savanna
- Semi-desert and scrub
- Hot desert
- Wetland
- Mountain
- Tundra
- Ice
- Cultivation
- Urban

■ National capital
● Internal capital
⊙ Major city or town
○ Other town

International boundary

Internal boundary

2,490m
(7,988ft) · Height above or below sea level

See also main key on page 17.

1:13,300,000

0 · 200 · 400km

0 · 100 · 200 · 300 miles

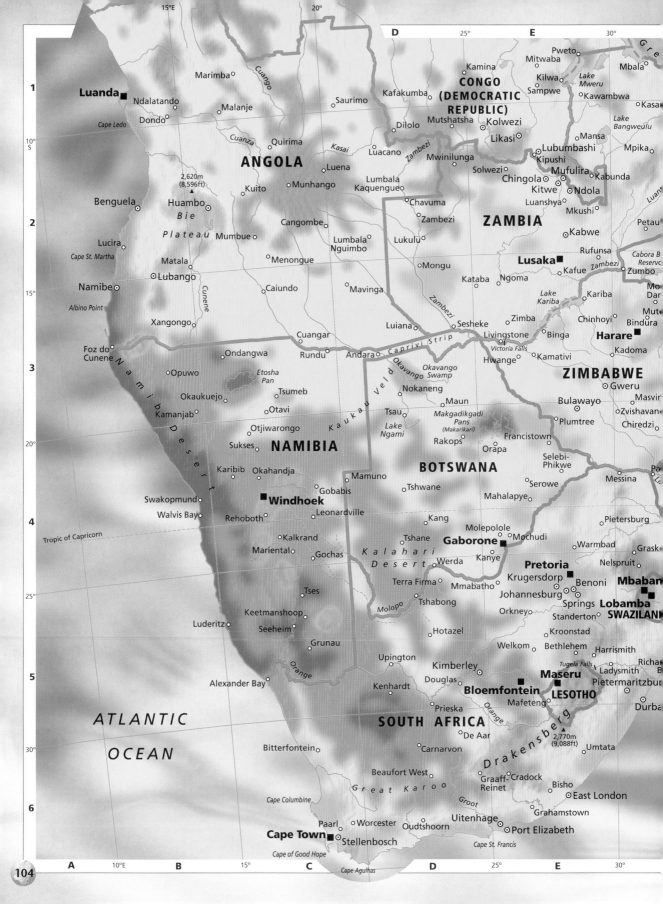

Mbeya
Makumbako
Ilonga
Njinjo
duma
Liwale
Karonga
TANZANIA
Lindi
Mtwara
Masasi
Songea
Tunduru
Palma
Mzuzu
Ruvuma
Cape Delgado
Mueda
Lupilichi
Mecula
Lake Nyasa
(Lake Malawi)
Lichinga
Nungo
Lilongwe
MALAWI
Cuamba
Zomba
Lake Chilwa
Nampula
Blantyre
Milange
Angoche
Zambezi
Mocuba
MOZAMBIQUE
Quelimane
ngani
92m
04ft)
tare
manimani
Beira
pungabera
Nova
Mambone
assangena
Bassas da India
(Reunion)
Chigubo
Barra Falsa Point
Massinga
Barra Point
Inhambane
Xai-Xai
aputo

SEYCHELLES
Aldabra Group
Providence
St. Pierre
Bancs Providence
Cosmoledo Group
Assumption
Farquhar Group
Astove

Grand Comoro
(Njazidja)
COMOROS
Glorioso Islands
(Reunion)
Moroni
Anjouan Island
(Nzwani)
Mutsamudu
Cape Amber
Fomboni
Mohilla Island
(Mwali)
Mamoudzou
Antsiranana
Mayotte
(France)
Ambilobe
Nosy Be
Ambanja
Bealanana
Analalava
Antalaha
Mahajanga
Mandritsara
Cape St. Andrew
Maroantsetra
Besalampy
Juan de Nova
(Reunion)
Maevatanana
Nosy Boraha
Ikopa
Toamasina
Antsalova
Tsiroanomandidy
Antananarivo
Belo-Tsiribihina
Mania
Antsirabe
Malaimbandy
Ambositra
MADAGASCAR
Morombe
Manja
Beroroha
Fianarantsoa
Ihosy
Manakara
▲2,658m
(8,720ft)
St. Denis
Reunion
(France)
Toliara
Betroka
Bekily
Tropic of Capricorn
Androka
Tolanaro
Cape St. Mary

INDIAN

OCEAN

St. Lucia

Nacala
Cape Melamo
Mozambique
Mozambique Channel
Pemba

Inset map (Mauritius)

INDIAN OCEAN
55°E
K   L
3   3
20°S   20°S
MAURITIUS
Port Louis
St. Denis
4   4
Reunion
(France)
K   L
Same scale as main map

Legend

Southern Africa

- Boreal forest
- Temperate forest
- Tropical forest
- Temperate grassland
- Savanna
- Semi-desert and scrub
- Hot desert
- — International boundary
- — Internal boundary
- ▲ 2,490m (7,988ft) Height above or below sea level

- Wetland
- Mountain
- Tundra
- Ice
- Cultivation
- Urban

- ■ National capital
- ● Internal capital
- ⊙ Major city or town
- ○ Other town

See also main key on page 17.

1:13,300,000

0   200   400km

0   100   200   300 miles

THE ARCTIC AND ANTARCTICA

T he Arctic and Antarctica are the world's coldest places. The Arctic is the area around the North Pole, including the Arctic Ocean and the most northerly parts of Europe, North America and Asia. Antarctica is a huge continent at the South Pole.

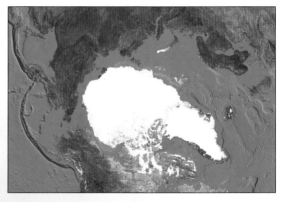

The large white area in this satellite image is ice, covering the Arctic Ocean and Greenland. At the top left of the image is the edge of Russia and at the top right is part of Europe.

Frozen island

Within the Arctic is Greenland, the world's largest island. Most Greenlanders live along the rocky coast, as the main body of land is covered in thick ice for most of the year.

This is the entrance to Sweden's Arctic ice hotel. The hotel is open in winter, then melts in the spring when the weather gets milder. The next winter, it is built all over again.

Internet links

For links to websites where you can explore the Arctic, watch video clips about life in Antarctica and meet animals that live at the opposite ends of the Earth, go to
www.usborne-quicklinks.com

A hotel of ice

Every winter, a hotel made entirely of ice is built in the far north of Sweden. Each piece of furniture is sculpted from ice, and even the beds are made of ice blocks. Guests sleep in special thermal sleeping bags with animal skins piled on top for extra warmth.

Icy continent

A huge, jagged sheet of ice permanently covers almost all of Antarctica, and spreads out over nearby seas as well. Scientists think that the area in the far west of the continent may be made up of many islands, but it is hard to tell because they are so far beneath the ice.

The darkest shading on this satellite image of Antarctica indicates ice that is over 3km (2 miles) deep.

Mountains run down the middle of Antarctica, and in the west there are volcanoes. Amazingly, one volcano heats the sea near it so much that it is warm enough to swim in.

These penguins are on the coast of Antarctica. They live in the ocean but come onto land to breed.

Life in Antarctica

The temperature in Antarctica can fall as low as -80°C (-112°F) in winter. It is too cold for people to live there, though scientists visit to study the area. No plants grow in the ice, and the only land animals are tiny mites. But many animals live in the seas around Antarctica, including penguins, seals, whales and fish.

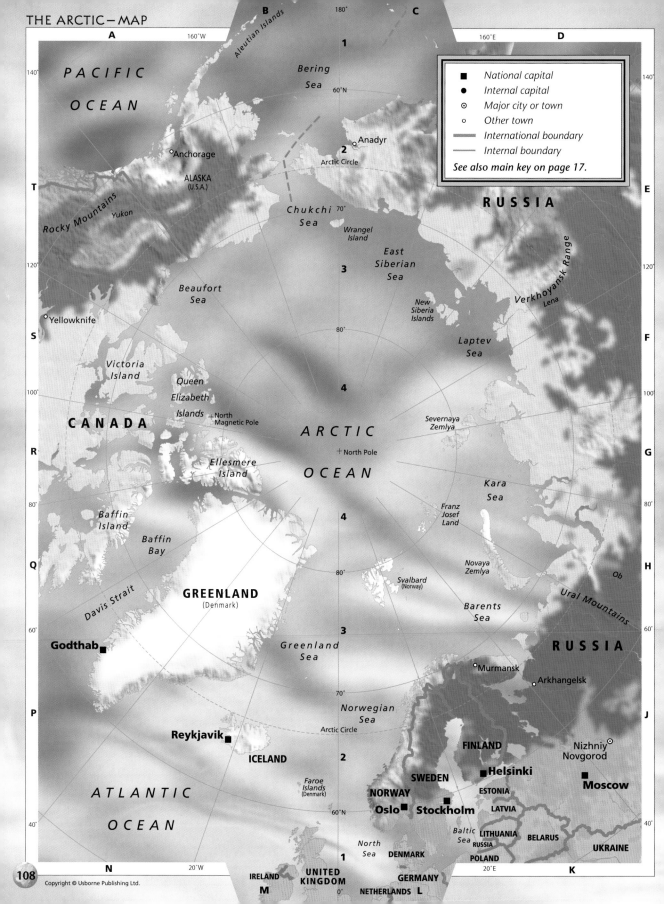

A   160°W   **B**   180°   **C**   160°E   **D**

■	National capital
●	Internal capital
⊙	Major city or town
○	Other town
▬	International boundary
▬	Internal boundary

See also main key on page 17.

PACIFIC OCEAN

Aleutian Islands

Bering Sea

60°N

Arctic Circle

○ Anchorage

ALASKA (U.S.A.)

Anadyr

RUSSIA

Chukchi Sea

70°

Rocky Mountains

Yukon

Wrangel Island

East Siberian Sea

Verkhoyansk Range

Lena

Beaufort Sea

New Siberia Islands

80°

○ Yellowknife

Laptev Sea

Victoria Island

Queen Elizabeth Islands

+ North Magnetic Pole

Severnaya Zemlya

CANADA

ARCTIC

Ellesmere Island

OCEAN

+ North Pole

Kara Sea

Baffin Island

Franz Josef Land

Baffin Bay

80°

Svalbard (Norway)

Novaya Zemlya

Ob

Davis Strait

GREENLAND (Denmark)

Barents Sea

Ural Mountains

RUSSIA

Godthab ■

Greenland Sea

70°

○ Murmansk

○ Arkhangelsk

Norwegian Sea

Arctic Circle

FINLAND

Nizhniy Novgorod ⊙

Reykjavik ■

ICELAND

SWEDEN

Helsinki ■

NORWAY

ESTONIA

Moscow ■

Faroe Islands (Denmark)

Oslo ■ Stockholm ■

LATVIA

ATLANTIC

Baltic Sea

LITHUANIA

BELARUS

OCEAN

60°N

RUSSIA

40°

North Sea

DENMARK

POLAND

20°E

UKRAINE

N   20°W   IRELAND   **M**   UNITED KINGDOM   0°   GERMANY   **L**   NETHERLANDS   **K**

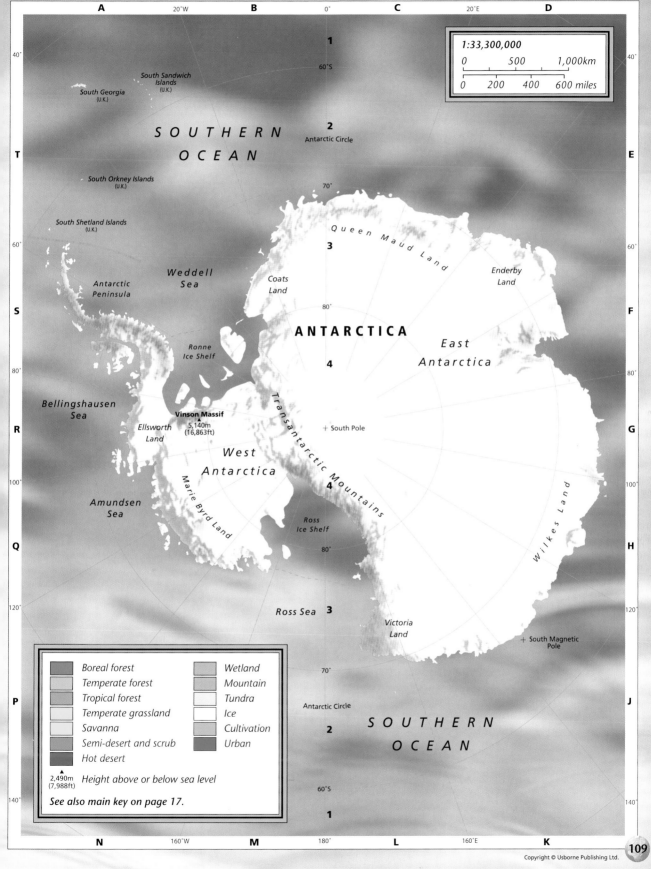

A 20°W B 0° C 20°E D

1
60°S

1:33,300,000
0 500 1,000km
0 200 400 600 miles

40° 40°

2
Antarctic Circle

SOUTHERN
OCEAN

T E

70°

South Georgia
(U.K.)

South Sandwich
Islands
(U.K.)

South Orkney Islands
(U.K.)

60° 60°

South Shetland Islands
(U.K.)

Queen Maud Land

3

Enderby
Land

Coats
Land

Weddell
Sea

Antarctic
Peninsula

80°

ANTARCTICA

East
Antarctica

S F

Ronne
Ice Shelf

80° 80°

Bellingshausen
Sea

Vinson Massif
5,140m
(16,863ft)

+ South Pole

Ellsworth
Land

West
Antarctica

R G

Transantarctic Mountains

4

Wilkes Land

100° 100°

Amundsen
Sea

Marie Byrd Land

4

Ross
Ice Shelf

80°

Q H

Ross Sea 3

120° 120°

Victoria
Land

+ South Magnetic
Pole

70°

Boreal forest
Temperate forest
Tropical forest
Temperate grassland
Savanna
Semi-desert and scrub
Hot desert

Wetland
Mountain
Tundra
Ice
Cultivation
Urban

Antarctic Circle

2

SOUTHERN
OCEAN

P J

2,490m
(7,988ft) Height above or below sea level

See also main key on page 17.

60°S

140° 140°

1

N 160°W M 180° L 160°E K

GEOGRAPHY QUIZ

Test your knowledge of the world's countries, cities, sights and animals with these quiz questions. The answers are on page 129.

The enormous, elaborate church above was designed by a famous Spanish architect named Antonio Gaudí.

Mystery places

Which famous sights are shown in the photographs on this page? Each has clues to help you.

The marble building on the left is one of the Seven Wonders of the World. It was built by an Indian emperor.

This famous steel bridge crosses the bay of a large North American city. It opened in 1937 and for many years was the longest suspension bridge in the world.

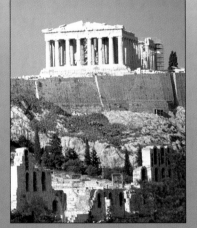

This city skyline is dominated by the tallest freestanding structure in the world. Visitors can go up the tower to a glass-bottomed viewing platform and a revolving restaurant. Can you name the tower and the city?

The ruins above are the remains of some of Europe's most important ancient temples and other public buildings.

Quick quiz

1. Which country's flag consists of a red circle on a white background?

2. When it is noon in Britain, what time is it in Mexico?

3. In which country is the Great Victoria Desert?

4. Which continent is the third-largest in the world?

5. In which country is Brno?

6. What is the world's deepest lake?

7. Name the smallest country in Europe.

8. Which country lies between Nicaragua and Panama?

9. In which country would you pay using naira and kobo as currency?

10. What is Turkey's capital city?

Internet links

For links to websites where you can try test-yourself quizzes and brush up your knowledge of world geography, go to **www.usborne-quicklinks.com**

Survival challenge

Could you survive in the world's toughest terrains? Take this test to find out.

1. Which of the following would not be very useful on a trip to Antarctica?
a) A warm hat and gloves
b) An umbrella
c) Sunglasses and sunscreen

2. You are in the Sahara Desert and are short of drinking water. What should you do?
a) Stay active, so you produce sweat to cool yourself down.
b) Put on extra clothes and rest as much as possible.
c) Talk and sing songs to keep yourself alert.

3. When on safari in Africa, which of these spiders should you avoid?
a) Six-eyed crab spiders
b) Button spiders
c) Violin spiders

4. You are walking in the Rocky Mountains and meet a grizzly bear. What should you do?
a) Lie on the ground and play dead.
b) Turn and run away as fast as possible.
c) Back away slowly and calmly.

This grizzly bear is in the Rocky Mountains in Utah, U.S.A. Grizzly bears like to keep well away from humans, but will occasionally attack if they feel threatened.

GAZETTEER OF STATES

Afghanistan

Albania

Algeria

Andorra

Angola

Antigua and Barbuda

• **Argentina**

This gazetteer lists the world's 193 independent states, along with key facts about each one. In the lists of languages, the language that is most widely spoken is given first, even if it is not the official language. In the lists of religions, the one followed by the most people is also placed first. Every state has a national flag, which is usually used to represent the country abroad. A few states also have a state flag which they prefer to use instead. The state flags appear here with a dot beside them.

AFGHANISTAN (Asia)
Area: 647,500 sq km (249,935 sq miles)
Population: 25,838,797
Capital city: Kabul
Main languages: Dari, Pashto
Main religion: Muslim
Government: transitional
Currency: 1 afghani = 100 puls

ALBANIA (Europe)
Area: 28,750 sq km (11,100 sq miles)
Population: 3,510,484
Capital city: Tirana
Main language: Albanian
Main religions: Muslim, Albanian Orthodox
Government: emerging democracy
Currency: 1 lek = 100 qintars

ALGERIA (Africa)
Area: 2,381,740 sq km (919,589 sq miles)
Population: 31,193,917
Capital city: Algiers
Main languages: Arabic, French, Berber dialects
Main religion: Sunni Muslim
Government: republic
Currency: 1 Algerian dinar = 100 centimes

ANDORRA (Europe)
Area: 468 sq km (181 sq miles)
Population: 67,627
Capital city: Andorra la Vella
Main languages: Catalan, Spanish
Main religion: Roman Catholic
Government: parliamentary democracy
Currency: 1 euro = 100 cents

ANGOLA (Africa)
Area: 1,246,700 sq km (481,351 sq miles)
Population: 10,366,031
Capital city: Luanda
Main languages: Kilongo, Kimbundu, other Bantu languages, Portuguese
Main religions: indigenous, Roman Catholic, Protestant
Government: transitional
Currency: 1 kwanza = 100 lwei

ANTIGUA AND BARBUDA (North America)
Area: 442 sq km (171 sq miles)
Population: 66,970
Capital city: Saint John's
Main languages: Caribbean Creole, English
Main religion: Protestant
Government: constitutional monarchy
Currency: 1 East Caribbean dollar = 100 cents

ARGENTINA (South America)
Area: 2,780,400 sq km (1,073,512 sq miles)
Population: 36,955,182
Capital city: Buenos Aires
Main language: Spanish
Main religion: Roman Catholic
Government: republic
Currency: 1 peso = 100 centavos

ARMENIA (Asia)
Area: 29,800 sq km (11,506 sq miles)
Population: 3,336,100
Capital city: Yerevan
Main language: Armenian
Main religion: Armenian Orthodox
Government: republic
Currency: 1 dram = 100 luma

AUSTRALIA (Australasia/Oceania)
Area: 7,686,850 sq km (2,967,124 sq miles)
Population: 19,357,594
Capital city: Canberra
Main language: English
Main religion: Christian
Government: federal democratic monarchy
Currency: 1 Australian dollar = 100 cents

AUSTRIA (Europe)
Area: 83,858 sq km (32,378 sq miles)
Population: 8,150,835
Capital city: Vienna
Main language: German
Main religion: Roman Catholic
Government: federal republic
Currency: 1 euro = 100 cents

Armenia

Australia

Austria

Azerbaijan

Bahamas, The

Bahrain

Bangladesh

Barbados

Belarus

Belgium

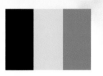

Belize

Benin

Bhutan

• **Bolivia**

AZERBAIJAN (Asia)
Area: 86,600 sq km (33,436 sq miles)
Population: 7,771,092
Capital city: Baku
Main language: Azeri
Main religion: Muslim
Government: republic
Currency: 1 manat = 100 gopiks

BAHAMAS, THE (North America)
Area: 13,940 sq km (5,382 sq miles)
Population: 297,852
Capital city: Nassau
Main languages: Bahamian Creole, English
Main religion: Christian
Government: parliamentary democracy
Currency: 1 Bahamian dollar = 100 cents

BAHRAIN (Asia)
Area: 678 sq km (261 sq miles)
Population: 645,361
Capital city: Manama
Main languages: Arabic, English
Main religion: Muslim
Government: traditional monarchy
Currency: 1 Bahraini dinar = 1,000 fils

BANGLADESH (Asia)
Area: 144,000 sq km (55,598 sq miles)
Population: 131,269,860
Capital city: Dhaka
Main languages: Bengali, English
Main religions: Muslim, Hindu
Government: republic
Currency: 1 taka = 100 poisha

BARBADOS (North America)
Area: 430 sq km (166 sq miles)
Population: 275,330
Capital city: Bridgetown
Main languages: Bajan, English
Main religion: Christian
Government: parliamentary democracy
Currency: 1 Barbadian dollar = 100 cents

BELARUS (Europe)
Area: 207,600 sq km (80,154 sq miles)
Population: 10,350,194
Capital city: Minsk
Main language: Belarusian
Main religion: Eastern Orthodox
Government: republic
Currency: 1 Belarusian ruble = 100 kopecks

BELGIUM (Europe)
Area: 30,510 sq km (11,780 sq miles)
Population: 10,258,762
Capital city: Brussels
Main languages: Dutch, French
Main religions: Roman Catholic, Protestant
Government: constitutional monarchy
Currency: 1 euro = 100 cents

BELIZE (North America)
Area: 22,960 sq km (8,865 sq miles)
Population: 256,062
Capital city: Belmopan
Main languages: Spanish, Belize Creole,
English, Garifuna, Maya

Main religions: Roman Catholic, Protestant
Government: parliamentary democracy
Currency: 1 Belizean dollar = 100 cents

BENIN (Africa)
Area: 112,620 sq km (43,483 sq miles)
Population: 6,590,782
Capital city: Porto-Novo
Main languages: Fon, French, Yoruba
Main religions: indigenous, Christian, Muslim
Government: republic
Currency: 1 CFA* franc = 100 centimes

BHUTAN (Asia)
Area: 47,000 sq km (18,146 sq miles)
Population: 2,049,412
Capital city: Thimphu
Main languages: Dzongkha, Nepali
Main religions: Muslim, Hindu
Government: monarchy
Currency: 1 ngultrum = 100 chetrum

BOLIVIA (South America)
Area: 1,098,580 sq km (424,162 sq miles)
Population: 8,300,463
Capital cities: La Paz, Sucre
Main languages: Spanish, Quechua, Aymara
Main religion: Roman Catholic
Government: republic
Currency: 1 boliviano = 100 centavos

BOSNIA AND HERZEGOVINA (Europe)
Area: 51,129 sq km (19,741 sq miles)
Population: 3,922,205
Capital city: Sarajevo
Main languages: Bosnian, Serbian, Croatian
Main religions: Muslim, Orthodox, Roman
Catholic
Government: emerging federal democracy
Currency: 1 marka = 100 pfenninga

BOTSWANA (Africa)
Area: 600,372 sq km (231,743 sq miles)
Population: 1,586,119
Capital city: Gaborone
Main languages: Setswana, Kalanga,
English
Main religions: indigenous, Christian
Government: parliamentary republic
Currency: 1 pula = 100 thebe

BRAZIL (South America)
Area: 8,547,400 sq km (3,300,151 sq miles)
Population: 174,468,575
Capital city: Brasilia
Main language: Portuguese
Main religion: Roman Catholic
Government: federal republic
Currency: 1 real = 100 centavos

BRUNEI (Asia)
Area: 5,770 sq km (2,228 sq miles)
Population: 343,653
Capital city: Bandar Seri Begawan
Main languages: Malay, English, Chinese
Main religions: Muslim, Buddhist
Government: constitutional sultanate (a type
of monarchy)
Currency: 1 Bruneian dollar = 100 cents

**Bosnia and
Herzegovina**

Botswana

Brazil

Brunei

Bulgaria

Burkina Faso

Burma (Myanmar)

113

GAZETTEER OF STATES CONTINUED:

Burundi

Cambodia

Cameroon

Canada

Cape Verde

Central African Republic

Chad

BULGARIA (Europe)
Area: 110,910 sq km (42,822 sq miles)
Population: 7,707,495
Capital city: Sofia
Main language: Bulgarian
Main religions: Bulgarian Orthodox, Muslim
Government: republic
Currency: 1 lev = 100 stotinki

BURKINA FASO (Africa)
Area: 274,200 sq km (105,869 sq miles)
Population: 12,272,289
Capital city: Ouagadougou
Main languages: Moore, Jula, French
Main religions: Muslim, indigenous
Government: republic
Currency: 1 CFA* franc = 100 centimes

BURMA (MYANMAR) (Asia)
Area: 678,500 sq km (261,969 sq miles)
Population: 50,438,300
Capital city: Rangoon
Main language: Burmese
Main religion: Buddhist
Government: military dictatorship
Currency: 1 kyat = 100 pyas

BURUNDI (Africa)
Area: 27,830 sq km (10,745 sq miles)
Population: 6,223,897
Capital city: Bujumbura
Main languages: Kirundi, French, Swahili
Main religions: Christian, indigenous
Government: republic
Currency: 1 Burundi franc = 100 centimes

CAMBODIA (Asia)
Area: 181,040 sq km (69,900 sq miles)
Population: 12,491,501
Capital city: Phnom Penh
Main language: Khmer
Main religion: Buddhist
Government: constitutional monarchy
Currency: 1 new riel = 100 sen

CAMEROON (Africa)
Area: 475,440 sq km (183,567 sq miles)
Population: 15,803,220
Capital city: Yaounde
Main languages: Cameroon Pidgin English, Ewondo, Fula, French, English
Main religions: indigenous, Christian, Muslim
Government: republic
Currency: 1 CFA* franc = 100 centimes

CANADA (North America)
Area: 9,970,610 sq km (3,849,653 sq miles)
Population: 31,592,805
Capital city: Ottawa
Main languages: English, French
Main religions: Roman Catholic, Protestant
Government: federal democracy
Currency: 1 Canadian dollar = 100 cents

CAPE VERDE (Africa)
Area: 4,033 sq km (1,557 sq miles)
Population: 405,163
Capital city: Praia
Main languages: Crioulo*, Portuguese

Main religions: Roman Catholic, Protestant
Government: republic
Currency: 1 Cape Verdean escudo = 100 centavos

CENTRAL AFRICAN REPUBLIC (Africa)
Area: 622,436 sq km (240,322 sq miles)
Population: 3,576,884
Capital city: Bangui
Main languages: Sangho, French
Main religions: indigenous, Christian, Muslim
Government: republic
Currency: 1 CFA* franc = 100 centimes

CHAD (Africa)
Area: 1,284,000 sq km (495,752 sq miles)
Population: 8,707,078
Capital city: Ndjamena
Main languages: Arabic, Sara, French
Main religions: Muslim, Christian, indigenous
Government: republic
Currency: 1 CFA* franc = 100 centimes

CHILE (South America)
Area: 756,626 sq km (292,133 sq miles)
Population: 15,328,467
Capital city: Santiago
Main language: Spanish
Main religions: Roman Catholic, Protestant
Government: republic
Currency: 1 Chilean peso = 100 centavos

CHINA (Asia)
Area: 9,596,960 sq km (3,705,386 sq miles)
Population: 1,273,111,290
Capital city: Beijing
Main languages: Mandarin Chinese, Yue, Wu
Main religions: Taoist, Buddhist
Government: Communist state
Currency: 1 yuan = 10 jiao

COLOMBIA (South America)
Area: 1,138,910 sq km (439,733 sq miles)
Population: 40,349,388
Capital city: Bogota
Main language: Spanish
Main religion: Roman Catholic
Government: republic
Currency: 1 Colombian peso = 100 centavos

COMOROS (Africa)
Area: 1,862 sq km (719 sq miles)
Population: 596,202
Capital city: Moroni
Main languages: Comorian*, French, Arabic
Main religion: Sunni Muslim
Government: republic
Currency: 1 Comoran franc = 100 centimes

CONGO (Africa)
Area: 342,000 sq km (132,046 sq miles)
Population: 2,894,336
Capital city: Brazzaville
Main languages: Munukutuba, Lingala, French
Main religions: Christian, animist
Government: republic
Currency: 1 CFA* franc = 100 centimes

Chile

China

Colombia

Comoros

Congo

Congo (Democratic Republic)

Costa Rica

*CFA = Communaute Financiere Africaine; Comorian = a blend of Swahili and Arabic; Crioulo = a blend of Portuguese and West African

Croatia

Cuba

Cyprus

Czech Republic

Denmark

Djibouti

Dominica

CONGO (DEMOCRATIC REPUBLIC) (Africa)
Area: 2,345,410 sq km (905,563 sq miles)
Population: 53,624,718
Capital city: Kinshasa
Main languages: Lingala, Swahili, Kikongo, Tshiluba, French
Main religions: Roman Catholic, Protestant, Kimbanguist, Muslim
Government: transitional
Currency: 1 Congolese franc = 100 centimes

COSTA RICA (North America)
Area: 51,100 sq km (19,730 sq miles)
Population: 3,773,057
Capital city: San Jose
Main language: Spanish
Main religions: Roman Catholic, Evangelical
Government: democratic republic
Currency: 1 Costa Rican colon = 100 centimos

CROATIA (Europe)
Area: 56,538 sq km (21,829 sq miles)
Population: 4,334,142
Capital city: Zagreb
Main language: Croatian
Main religions: Roman Catholic, Orthodox
Government: parliamentary democracy
Currency: 1 kuna = 100 lipas

CUBA (North America)
Area: 110,860 sq km (42,803 sq miles)
Population: 11,184,023
Capital city: Havana
Main language: Spanish
Main religion: Roman Catholic
Government: Communist state
Currency: 1 Cuban peso = 100 centavos

CYPRUS (Europe)
Area: 9,250 sq km (3,571 sq miles)
Population: 762,887
Capital city: Nicosia
Main languages: Greek, Turkish
Main religions: Greek Orthodox, Muslim
Government: republic with a self-proclaimed independent Turkish area
Currency: Greek Cypriot area: 1 Cypriot pound = 100 cents; Turkish Cypriot area: 1 Turkish lira = 100 kurus

CZECH REPUBLIC (Europe)
Area: 78,866 sq km (30,450 sq miles)
Population: 10,264,212
Capital city: Prague
Main language: Czech
Main religion: Roman Catholic
Government: parliamentary democracy
Currency: 1 koruna = 100 haleru

DENMARK (Europe)
Area: 43,094 sq km (16,639 sq miles)
Population: 5,352,815
Capital city: Copenhagen
Main language: Danish
Main religion: Evangelical Lutheran
Government: constitutional monarchy
Currency: 1 Danish krone = 100 oere

DJIBOUTI (Africa)
Area: 23,200 sq km (8,957 sq miles)
Population: 460,700
Capital city: Djibouti
Main languages: Afar, Somali, Arabic, French
Main religion: Muslim
Government: republic
Currency: 1 Djiboutian franc = 100 centimes

DOMINICA (North America)
Area: 751 sq km (290 sq miles)
Population: 70,786
Capital city: Roseau
Main languages: English, French patois
Main religions: Roman Catholic, Protestant
Government: democratic republic
Currency: 1 East Caribbean dollar = 100 cents

DOMINICAN REPUBLIC (North America)
Area: 48,511 sq km (18,731 sq miles)
Population: 8,581,477
Capital city: Santo Domingo
Main language: Spanish
Main religion: Roman Catholic
Government: democratic republic
Currency: 1 Dominican peso = 100 centavos

EAST TIMOR (Asia)
Area: 24,000 sq km (9,266 sq miles)
Population: 737,811
Capital city: Dili
Main languages: Tetun (Tetum), Bahasa Indonesia, Portuguese
Main religions: Roman Catholic, animist
Government: republic
Currency: 1 U.S. dollar = 100 cents

ECUADOR (South America)
Area: 283,560 sq km (109,483 sq miles)
Population: 13,183,978
Capital city: Quito
Main languages: Spanish, Quechua
Main religion: Roman Catholic
Government: republic
Currency: 1 sucre = 100 centavos

EGYPT (Africa)
Area: 1,001,450 sq km (386,660 sq miles)
Population: 69,536,644
Capital city: Cairo
Main language: Arabic
Main religion: Sunni Muslim
Government: republic
Currency: 1 Egyptian pound = 100 piasters

EL SALVADOR (North America)
Area: 21,040 sq km (8,124 sq miles)
Population: 6,237,662
Capital city: San Salvador
Main language: Spanish
Main religion: Roman Catholic
Government: republic
Currency: 1 Salvadoran colon = 100 centavos

EQUATORIAL GUINEA (Africa)
Area: 28,050 sq km (10,830 sq miles)
Population: 486,060
Capital city: Malabo
Main languages: Fang, Bubi, other Bantu

• **Dominican Republic**

East Timor

• **Ecuador**

Egypt

• **El Salvador**

Equatorial Guinea

Eritrea

GAZETTEER OF STATES CONTINUED:

Estonia

Ethiopia

Federated States of Micronesia

Fiji

Finland

France

Gabon

languages, Spanish, French, Pidgin English
Main religion: Christian
Government: republic
Currency: 1 CFA* franc = 100 centimes

ERITREA (Africa)
Area: 117,600 sq km (45,405 sq miles)
Population: 4,298,269
Capital city: Asmara
Main languages: Tigrinya, Afar, Arabic
Main religions: Muslim, Coptic Christian, Roman Catholic, Protestant
Government: transitional
Currency: 1 nafka = 100 cents

ESTONIA (Europe)
Area: 45,226 sq km (17,462 sq miles)
Population: 1,423,316
Capital city: Tallinn
Main languages: Estonian, Russian
Main religions: Evangelical Lutheran, Russian and Estonian Orthodox, other Christian
Government: parliamentary democracy
Currency: 1 Estonian kroon = 100 senti

ETHIOPIA (Africa)
Area: 1,127,127 sq km (435,184 sq miles)
Population: 65,891,874
Capital city: Addis Ababa
Main languages: Amharic, Tigrinya, Arabic
Main religions: Muslim, Ethiopian Orthodox, animist
Government: federal republic
Currency: 1 birr = 100 cents

FEDERATED STATES OF MICRONESIA (Australasia/Oceania)
Area: 702 sq km (271 sq miles)
Population: 134,597
Capital city: Palikir
Main languages: Chuuk, Ponapean, English
Main religions: Roman Catholic, Protestant
Government: democracy
Currency: 1 U.S. dollar = 100 cents

FIJI (Australasia/Oceania)
Area: 18,270 sq km (7,054 sq miles)
Population: 844,330
Capital city: Suva
Main languages: Fijian, Hindustani, English
Main religions: Christian, Hindu
Government: republic
Currency: 1 Fijian dollar = 100 cents

FINLAND (Europe)
Area: 337,030 sq km (130,127 sq miles)
Population: 5,175,783
Capital city: Helsinki
Main language: Finnish
Main religion: Evangelical Lutheran
Government: republic
Currency: 1 euro = 100 cents

FRANCE (Europe)
Area: 547,030 sq km (211,208 sq miles)
Population: 59,551,227
Capital city: Paris
Main language: French

Main religion: Roman Catholic
Government: republic
Currency: 1 euro = 100 cents

GABON (Africa)
Area: 267,670 sq km (103,347 sq miles)
Population: 1,221,175
Capital city: Libreville
Main languages: Fang, Myene, French
Main religions: Christian, animist
Government: republic
Currency: 1 CFA* franc = 100 centimes

GAMBIA, THE (Africa)
Area: 11,300 sq km (4,363 sq miles)
Population: 1,411,205
Capital city: Banjul
Main languages: Mandinka, Fula, Wolof, English
Main religion: Muslim
Government: democratic republic
Currency: 1 dalasi = 100 butut

GEORGIA (Asia)
Area: 69,700 sq km (26,911 sq miles)
Population: 4,989,285
Capital city: Tbilisi
Main languages: Georgian, Russian
Main religions: Georgian Orthodox, Muslim, Russian Orthodox
Government: republic
Currency: 1 lari = 100 tetri

GERMANY (Europe)
Area: 357,021 sq km (137,846 sq miles)
Population: 83,029,536
Capital city: Berlin
Main language: German
Main religions: Protestant, Roman Catholic
Government: federal republic
Currency: 1 euro = 100 cents

GHANA (Africa)
Area: 238,540 sq km (92,100 sq miles)
Population: 19,894,014
Capital city: Accra
Main languages: Twi, Fante, Ga, Hausa, Dagbani, Ewe, Nzemi, English
Main religions: indigenous, Muslim, Christian
Government: democratic republic
Currency: 1 new cedi = 100 pesewas

GREECE (Europe)
Area: 131,940 sq km (50,942 sq miles)
Population: 10,623,835
Capital city: Athens
Main language: Greek
Main religion: Greek Orthodox
Government: parliamentary republic
Currency: 1 euro = 100 cents

GRENADA (North America)
Area: 340 sq km (131 sq miles)
Population: 89,227
Capital city: Saint George's
Main languages: English, French patois
Main religions: Roman Catholic, Protestant
Government: constitutional monarchy
Currency: 1 East Caribbean dollar = 100 cents

Gambia, The

Georgia

Germany

Ghana

Greece

Grenada

Guatemala

*CFA = Communaute Financiere Africaine

Guinea

Guinea-Bissau

Guyana

• **Haiti**

Honduras

Hungary

Iceland

GUATEMALA (North America)
Area: 108,890 sq km (42,042 sq miles)
Population: 12,974,361
Capital city: Guatemala City
Main languages: Spanish, Amerindian languages including Quiche, Kekchi, Cakchiquel, Mam
Main religions: Roman Catholic, Protestant, indigenous Mayan beliefs
Government: democratic republic
Currency: 1 quetzal = 100 centavos

GUINEA (Africa)
Area: 245,860 sq km (94,927 sq miles)
Population: 7,613,870
Capital city: Conakry
Main languages: Fuuta Jalon, Mallinke, Susu, French
Main religion: Muslim
Government: republic
Currency: 1 Guinean franc = 100 centimes

GUINEA-BISSAU (Africa)
Area: 36,120 sq km (13,946 sq miles)
Population: 1,315,822
Capital city: Bissau
Main languages: Crioulo*, Balante, Pulaar, Mandjak, Mandinka, Portuguese
Main religions: indigenous, Muslim
Government: republic
Currency: 1 CFA* franc = 100 centimes

GUYANA (South America)
Area: 214,970 sq km (83,000 sq miles)
Population: 697,181
Capital city: Georgetown
Main languages: Guyanese Creole, English, Amerindian languages, Caribbean Hindi
Main religions: Christian, Hindu
Government: republic
Currency: 1 Guyanese dollar = 100 cents

HAITI (North America)
Area: 27,750 sq km (10,714 sq miles)
Population: 6,964,549
Capital city: Port-au-Prince
Main languages: Haitian Creole, French
Main religions: Roman Catholic, Protestant, Voodoo
Government: republic
Currency: 1 gourde = 100 centimes

HONDURAS (North America)
Area: 112,090 sq km (43,278 sq miles)
Population: 6,406,052
Capital city: Tegucigalpa
Main language: Spanish
Main religion: Roman Catholic
Government: republic
Currency: 1 lempira = 100 centavos

HUNGARY (Europe)
Area: 93,030 sq km (35,919 sq miles)
Population: 10,106,017
Capital city: Budapest
Main language: Hungarian
Main religions: Roman Catholic, Calvinist
Government: parliamentary democracy
Currency: 1 forint = 100 filler

ICELAND (Europe)
Area: 103,000 sq km (39,768 sq miles)
Population: 277,906
Capital city: Reykjavik
Main language: Icelandic
Main religion: Evangelical Lutheran
Government: republic
Currency: 1 Icelandic krona = 100 aurar

INDIA (Asia)
Area: 3,287,590 sq km (1,269,339 sq miles)
Population: 1,029,991,145
Capital city: New Delhi
Main languages: Hindi, English, Bengali, Urdu, over 1,600 other languages and dialects
Main religions: Hindu, Muslim
Government: federal republic
Currency: 1 Indian rupee = 100 paise

INDONESIA (Asia)
Area: 1,919,440 sq km (741,096 sq miles)
Population: 228,437,870
Capital city: Jakarta
Main languages: Bahasa Indonesia, English, Dutch, Javanese
Main religion: Muslim
Government: republic
Currency: 1 Indonesian rupiah = 100 sen

IRAN (Asia)
Area: 1,648,000 sq km (636,293 sq miles)
Population: 66,128,965
Capital city: Tehran
Main languages: Farsi and other Persian dialects, Azeri
Main religions: Shi'a Muslim, Sunni Muslim
Government: Islamic republic
Currency: 10 Iranian rials = 1 toman

IRAQ (Asia)
Area: 437,072 sq km (168,754 sq miles)
Population: 23,331,985
Capital city: Baghdad
Main languages: Arabic, Kurdish
Main religion: Muslim
Government: republic under a military regime
Currency: 1 Iraqi dinar = 1,000 fils

IRELAND (Europe)
Area: 70,280 sq km (27,135 sq miles)
Population: 3,840,838
Capital city: Dublin
Main languages: English, Irish (Gaelic)
Main religion: Roman Catholic
Government: republic
Currency: 1 euro = 100 cents

ISRAEL (Asia)
Area: 20,770 sq km (8,019 sq miles)
Population: 5,938,093
Capital city: Jerusalem
Main languages: Hebrew, Arabic
Main religions: Jewish, Muslim
Government: parliamentary democracy
Currency: 1 Israeli shekel = 100 agorot

ITALY (Europe)
Area: 301,230 sq km (116,305 sq miles)

India

Indonesia

Iran

Iraq

Ireland

Israel

Italy

*CFA = Communaute Financiere Africaine;
Crioulo = a blend of Portuguese and West African

GAZETTEER OF STATES CONTINUED:

Ivory Coast

Population: 57,679,825
Capital city: Rome
Main language: Italian
Main religion: Roman Catholic
Government: republic
Currency: 1 euro = 100 cents

IVORY COAST (Africa)
Area: 322,460 sq km (124,502 sq miles)
Population: 16,393,221
Capital city: Yamoussoukro
Main languages: Baoule, Dioula, French
Main religions: Christian, Muslim, animist
Government: republic
Currency: 1 CFA* = 100 centimes

Jamaica

JAMAICA (North America)
Area: 10,990 sq km (4,243 sq miles)
Population: 2,665,636
Capital city: Kingston
Main languages: Southwestern Caribbean Creole, English
Main religion: Protestant
Government: parliamentary democracy
Currency: 1 Jamaican dollar = 100 cents

Japan

JAPAN (Asia)
Area: 377,835 sq km (145,882 sq miles)
Population: 126,771,662
Capital city: Tokyo
Main language: Japanese
Main religions: Shinto, Buddhist
Government: constitutional monarchy
Currency: 1 yen = 100 sen

Jordan

JORDAN (Asia)
Area: 92,190 sq km (35,585 sq miles)
Population: 5,153,378
Capital city: Amman
Main languages: Arabic, English
Main religion: Sunni Muslim
Government: constitutional monarchy
Currency: 1 Jordanian dinar = 1,000 fils

Kazakhstan

KAZAKHSTAN (Asia)
Area: 2,717,300 sq km (1,049,150 sq miles)
Population: 16,731,303
Capital city: Astana
Main languages: Kazakh, Russian
Main religions: Muslim, Russian Orthodox
Government: republic
Currency: 1 Kazakhstani tenge = 100 tiyn

Kenya

KENYA (Africa)
Area: 582,650 sq km (224,961 sq miles)
Population: 30,765,916
Capital city: Nairobi
Main languages: Swahili, English, Bantu languages
Main religions: Christian, indigenous
Government: republic
Currency: 1 Kenyan shilling = 100 cents

Kiribati

KIRIBATI (Australasia/Oceania)
Area: 717 sq km (277 sq miles)
Population: 94,149
Capital city: Bairiki (on Tarawa island)
Main languages: Gilbertese, English
Main religions: Roman Catholic, Protestant

Government: republic
Currency: 1 Australian dollar = 100 cents

KUWAIT (Asia)
Area: 17,820 sq km (6,880 sq miles)
Population: 2,041,961
Capital city: Kuwait City
Main languages: Arabic, English
Main religion: Muslim
Government: monarchy
Currency: 1 Kuwaiti dinar = 1,000 fils

KYRGYZSTAN (Asia)
Area: 198,500 sq km (76,641 sq miles)
Population: 4,753,003
Capital city: Bishkek
Main languages: Kyrgyz, Russian
Main religions: Muslim, Russian Orthodox
Government: republic
Currency: 1 Kyrgyzstani som = 100 tyiyn

LAOS (Asia)
Area: 236,800 sq km (91,428 sq miles)
Population: 5,638,967
Capital city: Vientiane
Main languages: Lao, French, English
Main religions: Buddhist, animist
Government: Communist state
Currency: 1 new kip = 100 at

LATVIA (Europe)
Area: 64,589 sq km (24,938 sq miles)
Population: 2,385,231
Capital city: Riga
Main languages: Latvian, Russian
Main religions: Lutheran, Roman Catholic, Russian Orthodox
Government: parliamentary democracy
Currency: 1 Latvian lat = 100 santims

LEBANON (Asia)
Area: 10,400 sq km (4,015 sq miles)
Population: 3,627,774
Capital city: Beirut
Main languages: Arabic, French, English
Main religions: Muslim, Christian
Government: republic
Currency: 1 Lebanese pound = 100 piasters

LESOTHO (Africa)
Area: 30,350 sq km (11,718 sq miles)
Population: 2,177,062
Capital cities: Maseru, Lobamba
Main languages: Sesotho, English, Zulu, Xhosa
Main religions: Christian, indigenous
Government: constitutional monarchy
Currency: 1 loti = 100 lisente

LIBERIA (Africa)
Area: 111,370 sq km (43,000 sq miles)
Population: 3,225,837
Capital city: Monrovia
Main languages: Kpelle, English, Bassa
Main religions: indigenous, Christian, Muslim
Government: republic
Currency: 1 Liberian dollar = 100 cents

LIBYA (Africa)
Area: 1,759,540 sq km (679,358 sq miles)

Kuwait

Kyrgyzstan

Laos

Latvia

Lebanon

Lesotho

Liberia

*CFA = Communaute Financiere Africaine

Libya

Population: 5,240,599
Capital city: Tripoli
Main languages: Arabic, Italian, English
Main religion: Sunni Muslim
Government: military rule
Currency: 1 Libyan dinar = 1,000 dirhams

LIECHTENSTEIN (Europe)
Area: 160 sq km (62 sq miles)
Population: 32,528
Capital city: Vaduz
Main languages: German, Alemannic
Main religion: Roman Catholic
Government: constitutional monarchy
Currency: 1 Swiss franc = 100 centimes

Liechtenstein

LITHUANIA (Europe)
Area: 65,200 sq km (25,174 sq miles)
Population: 3,610,535
Capital city: Vilnius
Main languages: Lithuanian, Polish, Russian
Main religions: Roman Catholic, Lutheran, Russian Orthodox
Government: democracy
Currency: 1 Lithuanian litas = 100 centas

Lithuania

LUXEMBOURG (Europe)
Area: 2,586 sq km (998 sq miles)
Population: 442,972
Capital city: Luxembourg
Main languages: Luxemburgish, German, French
Main religion: Roman Catholic
Government: constitutional monarchy
Currency: 1 euro = 100 cents

Luxembourg

MACEDONIA (Europe)
Area: 25,333 sq km (9,781 sq miles)
Population: 2,046,209
Capital city: Skopje
Main languages: Macedonian, Albanian
Main religions: Macedonian Orthodox, Muslim
Government: emerging democracy
Currency: 1 Macedonian denar = 100 deni

Macedonia

MADAGASCAR (Africa)
Area: 587,040 sq km (226,656 sq miles)
Population: 15,982,563
Capital city: Antananarivo
Main languages: Malagasy, French
Main religions: indigenous beliefs, Christian
Government: republic
Currency: 1 Malagasy franc = 100 centimes

Madagascar

MALAWI (Africa)
Area: 118,480 sq km (45,745 sq miles)
Population: 10,548,250
Capital city: Lilongwe
Main languages: Chichewa, English
Main religions: Protestant, Roman Catholic, Muslim
Government: parliamentary democracy
Currency: 1 Malawian kwacha = 100 tambala

Malawi

MALAYSIA (Asia)
Area: 329,750 sq km (127,316 sq miles)
Population: 22,229,040
Capital city: Kuala Lumpur

Main languages: Bahasa Melayu, English, Chinese dialects, Tamil
Main religions: Muslim, Buddhist, Daoist
Government: constitutional monarchy
Currency: 1 ringgit = 100 sen

Malaysia

MALDIVES (Asia)
Area: 300 sq km (116 sq miles)
Population: 310,764
Capital city: Male
Main languages: Maldivian, English
Main religion: Sunni Muslim
Government: republic
Currency: 1 rufiyaa = 100 laari

Maldives

MALI (Africa)
Area: 1,240,000 sq km (478,764 sq miles)
Population: 11,008,518
Capital city: Bamako
Main languages: Bambara, Fulani, Songhai, French
Main religion: Muslim
Government: republic
Currency: 1 CFA* franc = 100 centimes

Mali

MALTA (Europe)
Area: 316 sq km (122 sq miles)
Population: 394,583
Capital city: Valletta
Main languages: Maltese, English
Main religion: Roman Catholic
Government: democratic republic
Currency: 1 Maltese lira = 100 cents

Malta

MARSHALL ISLANDS (Australasia/Oceania)
Area: 181 sq km (70 sq miles)
Population: 70,822
Capital city: Majuro
Main languages: Marshallese, English
Main religion: Protestant
Government: republic
Currency: 1 U.S. dollar = 100 cents

Marshall Islands

MAURITANIA (Africa)
Area: 1,030,700 sq km (397,953 sq miles)
Population: 2,747,312
Capital city: Nouakchott
Main languages: Arabic, Wolof, French
Main religion: Muslim
Government: republic
Currency: 1 ouguiya = 5 khoums

Mauritania

MAURITIUS (Africa)
Area: 1,860 sq km (718 sq miles)
Population: 1,189,825
Capital city: Port Louis
Main languages: Mauritius Creole French, French, Hindi, Bhojpuri, Urdu, Tamil, English
Main religions: Hindu, Christian, English
Government: parliamentary democracy
Currency: 1 Mauritian rupee = 100 cents

MEXICO (North America)
Area: 1,972,550 sq km (761,602 sq miles)
Population: 101,879,171
Capital city: Mexico City
Main languages: Spanish, Mayan, Nahuatl

Mauritius

*CFA = Communaute Financiere Africaine

GAZETTEER OF STATES CONTINUED:

Mexico

Main religion: Roman Catholic
Government: federal republic
Currency: 1 New Mexican peso = 100 centavos

MOLDOVA (Europe)
Area: 33,843 sq km (13,067 sq miles)
Population: 4,431,570
Capital city: Chisinau
Main languages: Moldovan, Russian, Gagauz
Main religion: Eastern Orthodox
Government: republic
Currency: 1 Moldovan leu = 100 bani

Moldova

MONACO (Europe)
Area: 1.95 sq km (0.75 sq miles)
Population: 31,842
Capital city: Monaco
Main languages: French, Monegasque, Italian
Main religion: Roman Catholic
Government: constitutional monarchy
Currency: 1 euro = 100 cents

Monaco

MONGOLIA (Asia)
Area: 1,565,000 sq km (604,247 sq miles)
Population: 2,654,999
Capital city: Ulan Bator
Main language: Khalkha Mongol
Main religion: Tibetan Buddist Lamaist
Government: republic
Currency: 1 tugrik = 100 mongos

Mongolia

MOROCCO (Africa)
Area: 446,550 sq km (172,413 sq miles)
Population: 30,645,305
Capital city: Rabat
Main languages: Arabic, Berber, French
Main religion: Muslim
Government: constitutional monarchy
Currency: 1 Moroccan dirham = 100 centimes

Morocco

MOZAMBIQUE (Africa)
Area: 801,590 sq km (309,494 sq miles)
Population: 19,371,057
Capital city: Maputo
Main languages: Makua, Tsonga, Portuguese
Main religions: indigenous, Christian, Muslim
Government: republic
Currency: 1 metical = 100 centavos

Mozambique

NAMIBIA (Africa)
Area: 825,418 sq km (318,694 sq miles)
Population: 1,797,677
Capital city: Windhoek
Main languages: Afrikaans, German, English
Main religions: Christian, indigenous
Government: republic
Currency: 1 Namibian dollar = 100 cents

Namibia

NAURU (Australasia/Oceania)
Area: 21 sq km (8 sq miles)
Population: 12,088
Capital: Yaren
Main languages: Nauruan, English
Main religion: Christian
Government: republic
Currency: 1 Australian dollar = 100 cents

NEPAL (Asia)
Area: 147,181 sq km (56,827 sq miles)
Population: 25,284,463
Capital city: Kathmandu
Main languages: Nepali, Maithili
Main religions: Hindu, Buddhist
Government: constitutional monarchy
Currency: 1 Nepalese rupee = 100 paisa

NETHERLANDS (Europe)
Area: 41,532 sq km (16,036 sq miles)
Population: 15,981,472
Capital cities: Amsterdam, The Hague
Main language: Dutch
Main religion: Christian
Government: constitutional monarchy
Currency: 1 euro = 100 cents

NEW ZEALAND (Australasia/Oceania)
Area: 268,680 sq km (103,737 sq miles)
Population: 3,864,129
Capital city: Wellington
Main languages: English, Maori
Main religion: Christian
Government: parliamentary democracy
Currency: 1 New Zealand dollar = 100 cents

NICARAGUA (North America)
Area: 129,494 sq km (49,998 sq miles)
Population: 4,918,393
Capital city: Managua
Main language: Spanish
Main religion: Roman Catholic
Government: republic
Currency: 1 gold cordoba = 100 centavos

NIGER (Africa)
Area: 1,267,000 sq km (489,189 sq miles)
Population: 10,355,156
Capital city: Niamey
Main languages: Hausa, Djerma, French
Main religion: Muslim
Government: republic
Currency: 1 CFA* franc = 100 centimes

NIGERIA (Africa)
Area: 923,768 sq km (356,667 sq miles)
Population: 126,635,626
Capital city: Abuja
Main languages: Hausa, Yoruba, Igbo, English
Main religions: Muslim, Christian, indigenous
Government: republic
Currency: 1 naira = 100 kobo

NORTH KOREA (Asia)
Area: 120,540 sq km (46,540 sq miles)
Population: 21,968,228
Capital city: Pyongyang
Main language: Korean
Main religions: Buddhist, Confucianist
Government: authoritarian socialist
Currency: 1 North Korean won = 100 chon

NORWAY (Europe)
Area: 324,220 sq km (125,181 sq miles)
Population: 4,503,440
Capital city: Oslo
Main language: Norwegian

Nauru

Nepal

Netherlands

New Zealand

Nicaragua

Niger

Nigeria

*CFA = Communaute Financiere Africaine

Main religion: Evangelical Lutheran
Government: constitutional monarchy
Currency: 1 Norwegian krone = 100 oere

OMAN (Asia)
Area: 212,460 sq km (82,031 sq miles)
Population: 2,622,198
Capital city: Muscat
Main languages: Arabic, English, Baluchi
Main religion: Muslim
Government: monarchy
Currency: 1 Omani rial = 1,000 baiza

PAKISTAN (Asia)
Area: 803,940 sq km (310,401 sq miles)
Population: 144,616,639
Capital city: Islamabad
Main languages: Punjabi, Sindhi, Urdu, English
Main religion: Muslim
Government: federal republic
Currency: 1 Pakistani rupee = 100 paisa

PALAU (Australasia/Oceania)
Area: 459 sq km (177 sq miles)
Population: 19,092
Capital city: Koror
Main languages: Palauan, English
Main religions: Christian, Modekngei
Government: democratic republic
Currency: 1 U.S. dollar = 100 cents

PANAMA (North America)
Area: 78,200 sq km (30,193 sq miles)
Population: 2,845,647
Capital city: Panama City
Main languages: Spanish, English
Main religions: Roman Catholic, Protestant
Government: democracy
Currency: 1 balboa = 100 centesimos

PAPUA NEW GUINEA (Australasia/Oceania)
Area: 462,840 sq km (178,703 sq miles)
Population: 5,049,055
Capital city: Port Moresby
Main languages: Tok Pisin, Hiri Motu, English
Main religions: Christian, indigenous
Government: parliamentary democracy
Currency: 1 kina = 100 toea

PARAGUAY (South America)
Area: 406,750 sq km (157,046 sq miles)
Population: 5,734,139
Capital city: Asuncion
Main languages: Guarani, Spanish
Main religion: Roman Catholic
Government: republic
Currency: 1 guarani = 100 centimos

PERU (South America)
Area: 1,285,220 sq km (496,223 sq miles)
Population: 27,483,864
Capital city: Lima
Main languages: Spanish, Quechua, Aymara
Main religion: Roman Catholic
Government: republic
Currency: 1 nuevo sol = 100 centimos

PHILIPPINES (Asia)
Area: 300,000 sq km (115,830 sq miles)
Population: 82,841,518
Capital city: Manila
Main languages: Tagalog, English, Ilocano
Main religion: Roman Catholic
Government: republic
Currency: 1 Philippine peso = 100 centavos

POLAND (Europe)
Area: 312,685 sq km (120,727 sq miles)
Population: 38,633,912
Capital city: Warsaw
Main language: Polish
Main religion: Roman Catholic
Government: democratic republic
Currency: 1 zloty = 100 groszy

PORTUGAL (Europe)
Area: 92,391 sq km (35,672 sq miles)
Population: 10,066,253
Capital city: Lisbon
Main language: Portuguese
Main religion: Roman Catholic
Government: democratic republic
Currency: 1 euro = 100 cents

QATAR (Asia)
Area: 11,437 sq km (4,416 sq miles)
Population: 769,152
Capital city: Doha
Main languages: Arabic, English
Main religion: Muslim
Government: monarchy
Currency: 1 Qatari riyal = 100 dirhams

ROMANIA (Europe)
Area: 237,500 sq km (91,699 sq miles)
Population: 22,364,022
Capital city: Bucharest
Main languages: Romanian, Hungarian, German
Main religion: Romanian Orthodox
Government: republic
Currency: 1 leu = 100 bani

RUSSIA (Europe and Asia)
Area: 17,075,200 sq km (6,592,735 sq miles)
Population: 145,470,197
Capital city: Moscow
Main language: Russian
Main religions: Russian Orthodox, Muslim
Government: federal government
Currency: 1 ruble = 100 kopeks

RWANDA (Africa)
Area: 26,338 sq km (10,169 sq miles)
Population: 7,312,756
Capital city: Kigali
Main languages: Kinyarwanda, French, English, Swahili
Main religions: Roman Catholic, Protestant, Adventist
Government: transitional
Currency: 1 Rwandan franc = 100 centimes

SAINT KITTS AND NEVIS (North America)
Area: 269 sq km (104 sq miles)
Population: 38,756

North Korea

Norway

Oman

Pakistan

Palau

Panama

Papua New Guinea

Paraguay

 Peru

Philippines

Poland

Portugal

Qatar

Romania

GAZETTEER OF STATES CONTINUED:

Russia

Capital city: Basseterre
Main language: English
Main religions: Protestant, Roman Catholic
Government: constitutional monarchy
Currency: 1 East Caribbean dollar = 100 cents

Rwanda

SAINT LUCIA (North America)
Area: 620 sq km (239 sq miles)
Population: 160,145
Capital city: Castries
Main languages: French patois, English
Main religion: Roman Catholic
Government: parliamentary democracy
Currency: 1 East Caribbean dollar = 100 cents

SAINT VINCENT AND THE GRENADINES
(North America)
Area: 389 sq km (150 sq miles)
Population: 116,394
Capital city: Kingstown
Main languages: English, French patois
Main religions: Protestant, Roman Catholic
Government: parliamentary democracy
Currency: 1 East Caribbean dollar = 100 cents

Saint Kitts and Nevis

SAMOA (Australasia/Oceania)
Area: 2,860 sq km (1,104 sq miles)
Population: 178,631
Capital city: Apia
Main languages: Samoan, English
Main religion: Christian
Government: constitutional monarchy
Currency: 1 tala = 100 sene

Saint Lucia

SAN MARINO (Europe)
Area: 61 sq km (24 sq miles)
Population: 27,730
Capital city: San Marino
Main language: Italian
Main religion: Roman Catholic
Government: republic
Currency: 1 euro = 100 cents

Saint Vincent and the Grenadines

SAO TOME AND PRINCIPE (Africa)
Area: 1,001 sq km (386 sq miles)
Population: 170,372
Capital city: Sao Tome
Main languages: Crioulo* dialects, Portuguese
Main religion: Christian
Government: republic
Currency: 1 dobra = 100 centimos

Samoa

SAUDI ARABIA (Asia)
Area: 1,960,582 sq km (756,987 sq miles)
Population: 23,513,330
Capital city: Riyadh
Main language: Arabic
Main religion: Muslim
Government: monarchy
Currency: 1 Saudi riyal = 100 halalah

• San Marino

SENEGAL (Africa)
Area: 196,190 sq km (75,749 sq miles)
Population: 10,589,571
Capital city: Dakar
Main languages: Wolof, French, Pulaar
Main religion: Muslim
Government: democratic republic
Currency: 1 CFA* franc = 100 centimes

SERBIA AND MONTENEGRO (Europe)
Area: 102,350 sq km (39,517 sq miles)
Population: 10,656,929
Capital city: Belgrade
Main language: Serbian
Main religions: Orthodox, Muslim
Government: republic
Currency: 1 Yugoslavian new dinar = 100 paras

SEYCHELLES (Africa)
Area: 455 sq km (176 sq miles)
Population: 80,098
Capital city: Victoria
Main languages: Seselwa, English, French
Main religion: Roman Catholic
Government: republic
Currency: 1 Seychelles rupee = 100 cents

SIERRA LEONE (Africa)
Area: 71,740 sq km (27,699 sq miles)
Population: 5,614,743
Capital city: Freetown
Main languages: Mende, Temne, Krio, English
Main religions: Muslim, indigenous, Christian
Government: constitutional democracy
Currency: 1 leone = 100 cents

SINGAPORE (Asia)
Area: 692 sq km (267 sq miles)
Population: 4,452,732
Capital city: Singapore
Main languages: Chinese, Malay, English, Tamil
Main religions: Buddhist, Muslim
Government: parliamentary republic
Currency: 1 Singapore dollar = 100 cents

SLOVAKIA (Europe)
Area: 48,845 sq km (18,859 sq miles)
Population: 5,422,366
Capital city: Bratislava
Main languages: Slovak, Hungarian
Main religion: Roman Catholic
Government: parliamentary democracy
Currency: 1 koruna = 100 halierov

SLOVENIA (Europe)
Area: 20,273 sq km (7,827 sq miles)
Population: 1,932,917
Capital city: Ljubljana
Main language: Slovenian
Main religion: Roman Catholic
Government: democratic republic
Currency: 1 tolar = 100 stotins

SOLOMON ISLANDS (Australasia/Oceania)
Area: 28,450 sq km (10,985 sq miles)
Population: 494,786
Capital city: Honiara
Main languages: Solomon pidgin, Kwara'ae,
To'abaita, English
Main religion: Christian
Government: parliamentary democracy
Currency: 1 Solomon Islands dollar = 100 cents

SOMALIA (Africa)
Area: 637,657 sq km (246,199 sq miles)
Population: 7,753,310
Capital city: Mogadishu
Main languages: Somali, Arabic, Oromo

Sao Tome and Principe

Saudi Arabia

Senegal

Serbia and Montenegro

Seychelles

Sierra Leone

Singapore

*CFA = Communaute Financiere Africaine; Crioulo = a
blend of Portuguese and West African

Slovakia

• **Slovenia**

Solomon Islands

Somalia

South Africa

South Korea

• **Spain**

Main religion: Sunni Muslim
Government: currently has no government
Currency: 1 Somali shilling = 100 cents

SOUTH AFRICA (Africa)
Area: 1,219,912 sq km (471,008 sq miles)
Population: 43,647,658
Capital cities: Pretoria, Cape Town, Bloemfontein
Main languages: Zulu, Xhosa, Afrikaans, Pedi, English, Tswana, Sotho, Tsonga, Swati, Venda, Ndebele
Main religions: Christian, indigenous
Government: republic
Currency: 1 rand = 100 cents

SOUTH KOREA (Asia)
Area: 98,480 sq km (38,023 sq miles)
Population: 48,324,000
Capital city: Seoul
Main language: Korean
Main religions: Christian, Buddhist
Government: republic
Currency: 1 South Korean won = 100 chun

SPAIN (Europe)
Area: 504,782 sq km (194,898 sq miles)
Population: 40,077,100
Capital city: Madrid
Main languages: Castilian Spanish, Catalan
Main religion: Roman Catholic
Government: constitutional monarchy
Currency: 1 euro = 100 cents

SRI LANKA (Asia)
Area: 65,610 sq km (25,332 sq miles)
Population: 19,576,783
Capital cities: Colombo, Sri Jayewardenepura Kotte
Main languages: Sinhala, Tamil, English
Main religions: Buddhist, Hindu
Government: republic
Currency: 1 Sri Lankan rupee = 100 cents

SUDAN (Africa)
Area: 2,505,810 sq km (967,493 sq miles)
Population: 37,090,298
Capital city: Khartoum
Main languages: Arabic, English
Main religions: Sunni Muslim, indigenous
Government: Islamic republic
Currency: 1 Sudanese dinar = 100 piastres

SURINAM (South America)
Area: 163,270 sq km (63,039 sq miles)
Population: 436,494
Capital city: Paramaribo
Main languages: Sranang Tongo, Dutch, English
Main religions: Christian, Hindu, Muslim
Government: constitutional democracy
Currency: 1 Surinamese guilder = 100 cents

SWAZILAND (Africa)
Area: 17,363 sq km (6,704 sq miles)
Population: 1,123,605
Capital cities: Mbabane, Lobamba

Main languages: Swati, English
Main religions: Christian, indigenous, Muslim
Government: monarchy
Currency: 1 lilangeni = 100 cents

SWEDEN (Europe)
Area: 449,964 sq km (173,731 sq miles)
Population: 8,876,744
Capital city: Stockholm
Main language: Swedish
Main religion: Lutheran
Government: constitutional monarchy
Currency: 1 Swedish krona = 100 oere

SWITZERLAND (Europe)
Area: 41,290 sq km (15,942 sq miles)
Population: 7,301,994
Capital city: Bern
Main languages: German, French, Italian
Main religions: Roman Catholic, Protestant
Government: federal republic
Currency: 1 Swiss franc = 100 centimes

SYRIA (Asia)
Area: 185,180 sq km (71,498 sq miles)
Population: 17,155,814
Capital city: Damascus
Main languages: Arabic, Kurdish
Main religions: Muslim, Christian
Government: republic under military regime
Currency: 1 Syrian pound = 100 piastres

TAIWAN (Asia)
Area: 35,980 sq km (13,892 sq miles)
Population: 22,548,009
Capital city: Taipei
Main languages: Taiwanese, Mandarin Chinese, Hakka Chinese
Main religions: Buddhist, Confucian, Daoist
Government: democracy
Currency: 1 New Taiwan dollar = 100 cents

TAJIKISTAN (Asia)
Area: 143,100 sq km (55,251 sq miles)
Population: 6,719,567
Capital city: Dushanbe
Main languages: Tajik, Russian
Main religion: Sunni Muslim
Government: republic
Currency: 1 somoni = 100 dirams

TANZANIA (Africa)
Area: 945,087 sq km (364,898 sq miles)
Population: 37,187,939
Capital cities: Dar es Salaam, Dodoma
Main languages: Swahili, English, Sukuma
Main religions: Christian, Muslim, indigenous
Government: republic
Currency: 1 Tanzanian shilling = 100 cents

THAILAND (Asia)
Area: 514,000 sq km (198,455 sq miles)
Population: 62,354,402
Capital city: Bangkok
Main languages: Thai, English, Chaochow
Main religion: Buddhist
Government: constitutional monarchy
Currency: 1 baht = 100 satang

Sri Lanka

Sudan

Surinam

Swaziland

Sweden

Switzerland

Syria

GAZETTEER OF STATES CONTINUED:

Taiwan

Tajikistan

Tanzania

Thailand

Togo

Tonga

TOGO (Africa)
Area: 56,785 sq km (21,925 sq miles)
Population: 5,285,501
Capital city: Lome
Main languages: Mina, Ewe, Kabye, French
Main religions: indigenous, Christian, Muslim
Government: republic
Currency: 1 CFA* franc = 100 centimes

TONGA (Australasia/Oceania)
Area: 748 sq km (289 sq miles)
Population: 106,137
Capital city: Nukualofa
Main languages: Tongan, English
Main religion: Christian
Government: constitutional monarchy
Currency: 1 pa'anga = 100 seniti

TRINIDAD AND TOBAGO (North America)
Area: 5,128 sq km (1,980 sq miles)
Population: 1,163,724
Capital city: Port-of-Spain
Main languages: English, French, Spanish, Hindi
Main religions: Christian, Hindu
Government: parliamentary democracy
Currency: 1 Trinidad and Tobago dollar = 100 cents

TUNISIA (Africa)
Area: 163,610 sq km (63,170 sq miles)
Population: 9,815,644
Capital city: Tunis
Main languages: Arabic, French
Main religion: Muslim
Government: republic
Currency: 1 Tunisian dinar = 1,000 millimes

TURKEY (Europe and Asia)
Area: 780,580 sq km (301,382 sq miles)
Population: 67,308,928
Capital city: Ankara
Main language: Turkish
Main religion: Muslim
Government: democratic republic
Currency: 1 Turkish lira = 100 kurus

TURKMENISTAN (Asia)
Area: 488,100 sq km (188,455 sq miles)
Population: 4,688,963
Capital city: Ashgabat (Ashkhabad)
Main languages: Turkmen, Russian
Main religion: Muslim
Government: republic
Currency: 1 Turkmen manat = 100 tenesi

TUVALU (Australasia/Oceania)
Area: 26 sq km (10 sq miles)
Population: 11,146
Capital city: Funafuti
Main languages: Tuvaluan, English
Main religion: Congregationalist
Government: constitutional monarchy
Currency: 1 Tuvaluan dollar or 1 Australian dollar = 100 cents

UGANDA (Africa)
Area: 236,040 sq km (91,135 sq miles)
Population: 24,699,073
Capital city: Kampala
Main languages: Luganda, English, Swahili
Main religion: Christian, Muslim, indigenous
Currency: 1 Ugandan shilling = 100 cents

UKRAINE (Europe)
Area: 603,700 sq km (233,089 sq miles)
Population: 48,396,470
Capital city: Kiev
Main languages: Ukrainian, Russian
Main religion: Ukrainian Orthodox
Government: republic
Currency: 1 hryvnia = 100 kopiykas

UNITED ARAB EMIRATES (Asia)
Area: 82,880 sq km (32,000 sq miles)
Population: 2,445,989
Capital city: Abu Dhabi
Main languages: Arabic, English
Main religion: Muslim
Government: federation
Currency: 1 Emirati dirham = 100 fils

UNITED KINGDOM (Europe)
Area: 244,820 sq km (94,525 sq miles)
Population: 59,778,002
Capital city: London
Main language: English
Main religions: Anglican, Roman Catholic
Government: constitutional monarchy
Currency: 1 British pound = 100 pence

UNITED STATES OF AMERICA (North America)
Area: 9,629,091 sq km (3,717,792 sq miles)
Population: 280,562,489
Capital city: Washington D.C.
Main language: English
Main religions: Protestant, Roman Catholic
Government: federal republic
Currency: 1 U.S. dollar = 100 cents

URUGUAY (South America)
Area: 176,220 sq km (68,039 sq miles)
Population: 3,386,575
Capital city: Montevideo
Main language: Spanish
Main religion: Roman Catholic
Government: republic
Currency: 1 Uruguayan peso = 100 centesimos

UZBEKISTAN (Asia)
Area: 447,400 sq km (172,741 sq miles)
Population: 25,563,441
Capital city: Tashkent
Main languages: Uzbek, Russian
Main religions: Muslim, Eastern Orthodox
Government: republic
Currency: 1 Uzbekistani sum = 100 tyyn

VANUATU (Australasia/Oceania)
Area: 12,189 sq km (4,706 sq miles)
Population: 196,178
Capital city: Port-Vila
Main languages: Bislama, French, English
Main religion: Christian
Government: republic
Currency: 1 vatu = 100 centimes

Trinidad and Tobago

Tunisia

Turkey

Turkmenistan

Tuvalu

Uganda

*CFA = Communaute Financiere Africaine

Ukraine

United Arab Emirates

United Kingdom

United States of America

Uruguay

Uzbekistan

VATICAN CITY (Europe)
Area: 0.44 sq km (0.17 sq miles)
Population: 900
Capital city: Vatican City
Main languages: Italian, Latin
Main religion: Roman Catholic
Government: led by the Pope
Currency: 1 euro = 100 cents

VENEZUELA (South America)
Area: 912,050 sq km (352,143 sq miles)
Population: 24,287,670
Capital city: Caracas
Main language: Spanish
Main religion: Roman Catholic
Government: federal republic
Currency: 1 bolivar = 100 centimos

VIETNAM (Asia)
Area: 329,560 sq km (127,243 sq miles)
Population: 81,098,416
Capital city: Hanoi
Main languages: Vietnamese, French, English, Khmer, Chinese
Main religion: Buddhist
Government: Communist state
Currency: 1 new dong = 100 xu

YEMEN (Asia)
Area: 527,970 sq km (203,849 sq miles)
Population: 18,701,257
Capital city: Sana
Main language: Arabic
Main religion: Muslim
Government: republic
Currency: 1 Yemeni rial = 100 fils

ZAMBIA (Africa)
Area: 752,614 sq km (290,584 sq miles)
Population: 9,959,037
Capital city: Lusaka
Main languages: Bemba, Tonga, Nyanja, English
Main religions: Christian, Muslim, Hindu
Government: republic
Currency: 1 Zambian kwacha = 100 ngwee

ZIMBABWE (Africa)
Area: 390,580 sq km (150,803 sq miles)
Population: 11,376,676
Capital city: Harare
Main languages: Shona, Ndebele, English
Main religions: Christian, indigenous
Government: republic
Currency: 1 Zimbabwean dollar = 100 cents

Vanuatu

Vatican City

Venezuela

Vietnam

Yemen

Zambia

Zimbabwe

The United Nations

The United Nations (U.N.) is an organization which aims to bring countries together to work for peace and development. Of the world's 193 states, 191 belong to the U.N. Those that don't belong are Taiwan and the Vatican City.

Kofi Annan, the Secretary-General of the U.N., with U.N. ambassador Pele

Internet links

For links to websites where you can match countries with their flags and find an online guide to the United Nations, go to
www.usborne-quicklinks.com

125

TIME ZONES

When it's midday in Rio de Janeiro, it's midnight in Tokyo. This is because the Earth is divided into different time zones. Within each zone, people usually set their clocks to the same time. If you fly between two zones, you change your watch to the time in the new zone.

Dividing up time

There are 25 main time zones. They are separated by one-hour intervals and there is a new time zone every 15 degrees of longitude. There are 12 one-hour zones both ahead of and behind Greenwich Mean Time, or GMT, which is the time at the Prime Meridian Line.

Governments can change their countries' time zones. So, for convenience, whole countries usually keep the same local time instead of sticking to the zones exactly. For example, China could be divided into several time zones, but instead the whole country keeps the same time. A few areas, such as India, use non-standard half hour deviations.

Summer time

Some countries adjust their clocks in summer. For example, in the U.K. all clocks go forward one hour. This is known as Daylight Saving Time or Summer Time. It is a way of getting more out of the days by having an extra hour of daylight in the evening. It reduces energy use as people don't use as much electricity for lights.

Changing dates

On the opposite side of the world from the Prime Meridian Line is the International Date Line, which runs mostly through the Pacific Ocean and bends to avoid the land. Places to the west of it are 24 hours ahead of places to the east. This means that if you travel east across it you lose a day and if you travel west across it you gain a day.

This map shows the time zones. The times at the top of the map tell you the time in the different zones when it is noon at the Prime Meridian Line. There are two midnight zones, one for each day on either side of the International Date Line. The numbers in circles tell you how many hours ahead of or behind Greenwich Mean Time an area is.

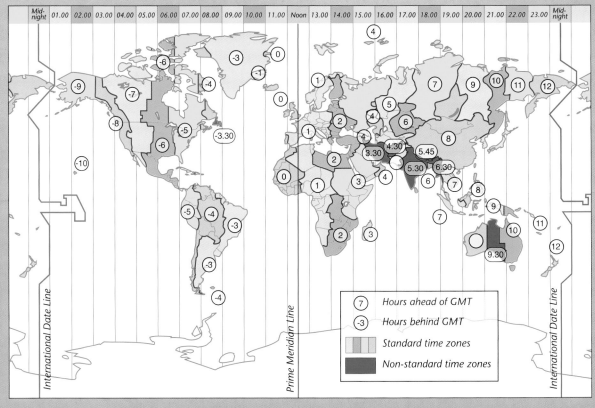

GENERAL INDEX

Places featured in the maps in this atlas are listed in a separate index on pages 130–143.

Answers to geography quiz (pages 110–111)

Mystery places

Top left: La Sagrada Familia church in Barcelona, Spain
Top right: The Taj Mahal near Agra, India
Middle left: The Golden Gate Bridge in San Francisco, U.S.A.
Middle right: The Acropolis in Athens, Greece
Bottom: The CN Tower in Toronto, Canada

Quick quiz

1. Japan
2. 6 a.m.
3. Australia
4. North America
5. Czech Republic
6. Lake Baikal, Russia
7. Vatican City
8. Costa Rica
9. Nigeria
10. Ankara

Survival challenge

1. b. An umbrella would not be useful as it doesn't rain in Antarctica. It's also the world's windiest continent, so an umbrella wouldn't last long! You would need sunglasses and sunscreen, however, as the reflection of the sun off snow is dazzling and can cause sunburn.

2. b. Extra clothes would help to conserve your sweat, which cools down your skin, and resting in the shade (if there is any) would help your body stay as cool as possible. Being active, talking or singing would cause your body to lose moisture and your mouth to dry out – which would make you even thirstier.

3. All of them. Six-eyed crab spiders are one of the most venomous types of spiders in the world. Their bites are so severe that they can cause death. Button spiders have a bite which is very painful, though not lethal, while a bite from a violin spider causes painful swelling.

4. c. A bear will only attack if it thinks you are a threat to it. If you moved away slowly, not making any sudden movements, it would probably leave you alone. You should only lie down (preferably curled into a ball) and play dead if the bear actually takes a swipe at you.

MAP INDEX

This is an index of the places and features named on the maps. Each entry consists of the following parts: the name (given in bold type), the country or region within which it is located (given in italics), the page on which the name can be found (given in bold type), and the grid reference (also given in bold type). For some names, there is also a description explaining what kind of place it is – for example a country, internal administrative area (state or province), national capital or internal capital. To find a place on a map, first find the map indicated by the page reference. Then use the grid reference to find the square containing the name or town symbol. See page 11 for help with using the grid.

Florencia, *Colombia,* 42 C3
Flores, *Azores,* 100 J10
Flores, *Indonesia,* 65 F5
Flores Sea, *Indonesia,* 65 F5
Floresta, *Brazil,* 43 L5
Floriano, *Brazil,* 43 K5
Florianopolis, *Brazil,* 44 J5
Florida, *U.S.A., internal admin. area,* 33 K5
Florida Keys, *U.S.A.,* 33 K6
Florida, Straits of, *North America,* 33 K6
Focsani, *Romania,* 91 H2
Foggia, *Italy,* 90 E3
Fogo, *Cape Verde,* 101 M12
Fomboni, *Comoros,* 105 H2
Formosa, *Argentina,* 44 G5
Fort Albany, *Canada,* 31 L3
Fortaleza, *Brazil,* 43 L4
Fort Chipewyan, *Canada,* 30 H3
Fort-de-France, *Martinique,* 34 M5
Fort Lauderdale, *U.S.A.,* 33 K5
Fort McMurray, *Canada,* 30 H3
Fort Nelson, *Canada,* 30 G3
Fort Peck Lake, *U.S.A.,* 32 E1
Fort Providence, *Canada,* 30 H2
Fort Severn, *Canada,* 31 L3
Fort Vermilion, *Canada,* 30 H3
Fort Wayne, *U.S.A.,* 33 J2
Fort Worth, *U.S.A.,* 32 G4
Foumban, *Cameroon,* 102 B2
Foxe Basin, *Canada,* 31 M2
Foxe Peninsula, *Canada,* 31 M2
Fox Islands, *U.S.A.,* 31 C3
Foz do Cunene, *Angola,* 104 B3
Foz do Iguacu, *Brazil,* 44 H5
France, *Europe, country,* 89 E5
Franceville, *Gabon,* 102 B4
Francistown, *Botswana,* 104 E4
Frankfort, *U.S.A., internal capital,* 33 K3
Frankfurt, *Germany,* 88 G4
Franz Josef Land, *Russia,* 74 C1
Fraser Island, *Australia,* 55 K5
Fredericton, *Canada, internal capital,* 31 N4
Fredrikstad, *Norway,* 86 D4
Freeport City, *The Bahamas,* 33 L5
Freetown, *Sierra Leone, national capital,* 101 C7
Freiburg, *Germany,* 88 F4
French Guiana, *South America, dependency,* 43 H3
French Polynesia, *Oceania, dependency,* 53 J6
Fresno, *U.S.A.,* 32 C3
Frisian Islands, *Europe,* 88 F3
Froya, *Norway,* 86 D3
Fuerteventura, *Canary Islands,* 100 B3
Fuji, Mount, *Japan,* 69 N3
Fukui, *Japan,* 69 N3
Fukuoka, *Japan,* 69 M4
Fukushima, *Japan,* 69 P3
Funafuti, *Tuvalu, national capital,* 52 E5
Funchal, *Madeira,* 100 B2
Furnas Reservoir, *Brazil,* 44 J4
Fushun, *China,* 69 K2
Fuxin, *China,* 69 K2
Fyn, *Denmark,* 87 D5

g

Gabes, *Tunisia,* 98 D2
Gabes, Gulf of, *Africa,* 98 D2
Gabon, *Africa, country,* 102 B4
Gaborone, *Botswana, national capital,* 104 E4
Gafsa, *Tunisia,* 98 C2
Gagnoa, *Ivory Coast,* 101 D7
Gairdner, Lake, *Australia,* 54 F6
Galapagos Islands, *Ecuador,* 42 N9
Galati, *Romania,* 91 J2
Galdhopiggen, *Norway,* 86 D3
Galle, *Sri Lanka,* 71 E9
Gallinas, Cape, *Colombia,* 42 D1
Galveston, *U.S.A.,* 33 H5
Galway, *Ireland,* 88 B3
Gambela, *Ethiopia,* 103 F2

Gambia, The, *Africa, country,* 101 B6
Ganca, *Azerbaijan,* 72 E3
Gander, *Canada,* 31 P4
Ganges, *Asia,* 70 E5
Ganges, Mouths of the, *Asia,* 71 F6
Ganzhou, *China,* 69 H5
Gao, *Mali,* 101 F5
Garda, Lake, *Italy,* 90 D2
Garissa, *Kenya,* 103 H4
Garonne, *France,* 89 E5
Garoua, *Cameroon,* 102 B2
Gaspe, *Canada,* 31 N4
Gatchina, *Russia,* 86 J4
Gavle, *Sweden,* 86 F3
Gaza, *Israel,* 73 B5
Gaziantep, *Turkey,* 72 C4
Gdansk, *Poland,* 87 F5
Gdansk, Gulf of, *Poland,* 87 F5
Gdynia, *Poland,* 87 F5
Gedaref, *Sudan,* 99 J6
Geelong, *Australia,* 54 H7
Gejiu, *China,* 68 F6
Gemena, *Democratic Republic of Congo,* 102 C3
General Roca, *Argentina,* 45 E7
General Santos, *Philippines,* 67 J6
General Villegas, *Argentina,* 44 F7
Geneva, *Switzerland,* 90 C2
Geneva, Lake, *Europe,* 90 C2
Genoa, *Italy,* 90 D2
Genoa, Gulf of, *Italy,* 90 D2
Gent, *Belgium,* 88 E4
Georgetown, *Guyana, national capital,* 43 G2
George Town, *Malaysia,* 64 B2
Georgia, *Asia, country,* 72 D3
Georgia, *U.S.A., internal admin. area,* 33 K4
Gera, *Germany,* 88 H4
Geraldton, *Australia,* 54 B5
Gerlachovsky stit, *Slovakia,* 87 G6
Germany, *Europe, country,* 88 G4
Gerona, *Spain,* 89 E6
Ghadamis, *Libya,* 98 C2
Ghana, *Africa, country,* 101 E7
Ghardaia, *Algeria,* 100 F2
Gharyan, *Libya,* 98 D2
Ghat, *Libya,* 98 D3
Gibraltar, *Europe,* 89 C7
Gibson Desert, *Australia,* 54 E4
Gijon, *Spain,* 89 C6
Gilbert Islands, *Kiribati,* 52 E5
Gilgit, *Pakistan,* 70 C3
Girardeau, Cape, *U.S.A.,* 33 J3
Giza, Pyramids of, *Egypt,* 99 H3
Gladstone, *Australia,* 55 K4
Glama, *Norway,* 86 D3
Glasgow, *United Kingdom,* 88 C3
Glazov, *Russia,* 85 G2
Glorioso Islands, *Africa,* 105 J2
Gloucester, *United Kingdom,* 88 D4
Gobabis, *Namibia,* 104 C4
Gobi Desert, *Asia,* 68 F2
Gochas, *Namibia,* 104 C4
Godavari, *India,* 71 D7
Gode, *Ethiopia,* 103 H2
Goiania, *Brazil,* 44 J3
Gold Coast, *Australia,* 55 K5
Golmud, *China,* 70 G3
Goma, *Democratic Republic of Congo,* 102 E4
Gonaives, *Haiti,* 35 K4
Gonder, *Ethiopia,* 103 G1
Gongga Shan, *China,* 68 F5
Good Hope, Cape of, *South Africa,* 104 C6
Goose Lake, *U.S.A.,* 32 B2
Gorakhpur, *India,* 71 E5
Gorgan, *Iran,* 72 F4
Gori, *Georgia,* 72 D3
Gorki Reservoir, *Russia,* 84 E2
Gorontalo, *Indonesia,* 65 F3
Gorzow Wielkopolski, *Poland,* 87 E5
Gothenburg, *Sweden,* 87 E4
Gotland, *Sweden,* 87 F4
Gottingen, *Germany,* 88 G4

Gouin Reservoir, *Canada,* 33 L1
Goundam, *Mali,* 101 E5
Governador Valadares, *Brazil,* 44 K3
Graaff-Reinet, *South Africa,* 104 D6
Grafton, *Australia,* 55 K5
Grahamstown, *South Africa,* 104 E6
Granada, *Spain,* 89 D7
Gran Canaria, *Canary Islands,* 100 B3
Gran Chaco, *South America,* 44 F4
Grand Bahama, *The Bahamas,* 33 L5
Grand Canal, *China,* 69 J4
Grand Canyon, *U.S.A.,* 32 D3
Grand Comoro, *Comoros,* 105 H2
Grande Bay, *Argentina,* 45 E10
Grande Prairie, *Canada,* 30 H3
Grand Forks, *U.S.A.,* 33 G1
Grand Island, *U.S.A.,* 32 G2
Grand Junction, *U.S.A.,* 32 E3
Grand Rapids, *Canada,* 31 K3
Grand Rapids, *U.S.A.,* 33 J2
Grand Teton, *U.S.A.,* 32 D2
Graskop, *South Africa,* 104 F5
Graz, *Austria,* 90 E2
Great Australian Bight, *Australia,* 54 F6
Great Barrier Reef, *Australia,* 54 J3
Great Basin, *U.S.A.,* 32 C2
Great Bear Lake, *Canada,* 30 G2
Great Dividing Range, *Australia,* 55 J6
Great Eastern Erg, *Algeria,* 100 G3
Greater Antilles, *North America,* 35 J4
Greater Khingan Range, *China,* 69 J1
Greater Sunda Islands, *Asia,* 64 C4
Great Falls, *U.S.A.,* 32 D1
Great Inagua, *The Bahamas,* 35 K3
Great Karoo, *South Africa,* 104 D6
Great Plains, *U.S.A.,* 32 F2
Great Rift Valley, *Africa,* 103 F5
Great Salt Desert, *Iran,* 72 F5
Great Salt Lake, *U.S.A.,* 32 D2
Great Salt Lake Desert, *U.S.A.,* 32 D2
Great Sandy Desert, *Australia,* 54 D4
Great Slave Lake, *Canada,* 30 H2
Great Victoria Desert, *Australia,* 54 D5
Great Wall of China, *China,* 68 F3
Great Western Erg, *Algeria,* 100 E2
Greece, *Europe, country,* 91 G4
Green Bay, *U.S.A.,* 33 J2
Greenland, *North America, dependency,* 108 P3
Greenland Sea, *Atlantic Ocean,* 108 M3
Greensboro, *U.S.A.,* 33 L3
Greenville, *U.S.A.,* 33 H4
Grenada, *North America, country,* 34 M5
Grenoble, *France,* 89 F5
Griffith, *Australia,* 54 J6
Groningen, *Netherlands,* 88 F3
Groot, *South Africa,* 104 D6
Groote Eylandt, *Australia,* 54 G2
Grossglockner, *Austria,* 90 E2
Groznyy, *Russia,* 72 E3
Grudziadz, *Poland,* 87 F5
Grunau, *Namibia,* 104 C5
Grytviken, *South Georgia,* 45 L10
Guadalajara, *Mexico,* 34 D3
Guadalquivir, *Spain,* 89 C7
Guadalupe Island, *Mexico,* 34 A2
Guadeloupe, *North America,* 34 M4
Guadiana, *Europe,* 89 C7
Gualeguaychu, *Argentina,* 44 G6
Guam, *Oceania,* 52 B3
Guangzhou, *China,* 69 H6
Guantanamo, *Cuba,* 35 J3
Guarapuava, *Brazil,* 44 H5
Guardafui, Cape, *Somalia,* 103 K1
Guatemala, *North America, country,* 34 F4
Guatemala City, *Guatemala, national capital,* 34 F5
Guaviare, *Colombia,* 42 E3
Guayaquil, *Ecuador,* 42 C4
Guayaquil, Gulf of, *Ecuador,* 42 B4
Gueckedou, *Guinea,* 101 C7
Guelma, *Algeria,* 90 C7
Guiana Highlands, *Venezuela,* 42 E2
Guilin, *China,* 68 H5
Guinea, *Africa, country,* 101 C6

Guinea-Bissau, *Africa, country,* 101 B6
Guinea, Gulf of, *Africa,* 101 F8
Guiria, *Venezuela,* 42 F1
Guiyang, *China,* 68 G5
Gujranwala, *Pakistan,* 70 C4
Gujrat, *Pakistan,* 70 C4
Gulbarga, *India,* 71 D7
Gulf, The, *Asia,* 73 F6
Gulu, *Uganda,* 103 F3
Gunung Kerinci, *Indonesia,* 64 B4
Gunung Tahan, *Malaysia,* 64 B3
Gurupi, *Brazil,* 44 J2
Gusau, *Nigeria,* 101 G6
Guwahati, *India,* 70 G5
Guyana, *South America, country,* 43 G2
Gwalior, *India,* 70 D5
Gweru, *Zimbabwe,* 104 E3
Gympie, *Australia,* 55 K5
Gyor, *Hungary,* 87 F7

h

Haapsalu, *Estonia,* 86 G4
Haarlem, *Netherlands,* 88 F3
Hadhramaut, *Yemen,* 73 E9
Ha Giang, *Vietnam,* 66 E3
Hague, The, *Netherlands, national capital,* 88 F3
Haifa, *Israel,* 72 B5
Haikou, *China,* 68 H6
Hail, *Saudi Arabia,* 73 D6
Hailar, *China,* 69 J1
Hainan, *China,* 68 H7
Hai Phong, *Vietnam,* 66 E3
Haiti, *North America, country,* 35 K4
Hakodate, *Japan,* 69 P2
Halifax, *Canada, internal capital,* 31 N4
Halmahera, *Indonesia,* 65 G3
Halmstad, *Sweden,* 87 E4
Hamadan, *Iran,* 72 E5
Hamah, *Syria,* 72 C4
Hamamatsu, *Japan,* 69 N4
Hamburg, *Germany,* 88 G3
Hameenlinna, *Finland,* 86 H3
Hamhung, *North Korea,* 69 L3
Hami, *China,* 70 G2
Hamilton, *Canada,* 31 M4
Hamilton, *New Zealand,* 55 Q7
Hammerfest, *Norway,* 86 G1
Handan, *China,* 69 H3
Hangzhou, *China,* 69 K4
Hannover, *Germany,* 88 G3
Hanoi, *Vietnam, national capital,* 66 E3
Happy Valley-Goose Bay, *Canada,* 31 N3
Haradh, *Saudi Arabia,* 73 E7
Harare, *Zimbabwe, national capital,* 104 F3
Harbin, *China,* 69 L1
Harer, *Ethiopia,* 103 H2
Hargeysa, *Somalia,* 103 H2
Harney Basin, *U.S.A.,* 32 C2
Harper, *Liberia,* 101 D8
Harrisburg, *U.S.A., internal capital,* 33 L2
Harrismith, *South Africa,* 104 E5
Hartford, *U.S.A., internal capital,* 33 M2
Hatteras, Cape, *U.S.A.,* 33 L3
Hattiesburg, *U.S.A.,* 33 J4
Hat Yai, *Thailand,* 66 D6
Hauki Lake, *Finland,* 86 J3
Havana, *Cuba, national capital,* 35 H3
Hawaii, *Pacific Ocean, internal admin. area,* 33 P7
Hawaiian Islands, *Pacific Ocean,* 33 P7
Hebrides, *United Kingdom,* 88 C2
Hefei, *China,* 69 J4
Hegang, *China,* 69 M1
Hejaz, *Saudi Arabia,* 73 C6
Helena, *U.S.A., internal capital,* 32 D1
Helmand, *Asia,* 70 B4
Helsingborg, *Sweden,* 87 E4
Helsinki, *Finland, national capital,* 86 H3
Hengyang, *China,* 68 H5
Henzada, *Burma,* 66 C4
Herat, *Afghanistan,* 70 A4
Hermosillo, *Mexico,* 34 B2
Hiiumaa, *Estonia,* 86 G4
Hilo, *U.S.A.,* 33 P8

Liverpool, *United Kingdom,* 88 D3
Livingstone, *Zambia,* 104 E3
Livorno, *Italy,* 90 D3
Liwale, *Tanzania,* 103 G5
Ljubljana, *Slovenia, national capital,*
  90 E2
Llanos, *South America,* 42 D2
Lloydminster, *Canada,* 30 J3
Lobamba, *Lesotho, national capital,*
  104 F5
Lodz, *Poland,* 87 F6
Lofoten, *Norway,* 86 E1
Logan, Mount, *Canada,* 30 F2
Logrono, *Spain,* 89 D6
Loire, *France,* 88 E5
Loja, *Ecuador,* 42 C4
Lokan Reservoir, *Finland,* 86 H2
Lolland, *Denmark,* 87 D5
Lombok, *Indonesia,* 64 E5
Lome, *Togo, national capital,* 101 F7
London, *Canada,* 31 L4
London, *United Kingdom, national capital,*
  88 D4
Londonderry, *United Kingdom,* 88 C3
Londrina, *Brazil,* 44 H4
Long Island, *The Bahamas,* 33 L6
Long Xuyen, *Vietnam,* 66 E5
Lopez, Cape, *Gabon,* 102 A4
Lop Lake, *China,* 70 G2
Lord Howe Island, *Australia,* 55 L6
Los Angeles, *Chile,* 45 D7
Los Angeles, *U.S.A.,* 32 C4
Los Mochis, *Mexico,* 34 C2
Louangphrabang, *Laos,* 66 D4
Loubomo, *Congo,* 102 B4
Louga, *Senegal,* 101 B5
Louisiana, *U.S.A., internal admin. area,*
  33 H4
Lower California, *Mexico,* 34 B2
Loyalty Islands, *New Caledonia,* 55 N4
Luacano, *Angola,* 104 D2
Luanda, *Angola, national capital,* 104 B1
Luangwa, *Africa,* 104 F2
Luanshya, *Zambia,* 104 E2
Lubango, *Angola,* 104 B2
Lubbock, *U.S.A.,* 32 F4
Lublin, *Poland,* 87 G6
Lubny, *Ukraine,* 84 C3
Lubumbashi, *Democratic Republic of*
  Congo, 102 E6
Lucena, *Philippines,* 67 H5
Lucerne, *Switzerland,* 90 D2
Lucira, *Angola,* 104 B2
Lucknow, *India,* 70 E5
Luderitz, *Namibia,* 104 C5
Ludhiana, *India,* 70 D4
Ludza, *Latvia,* 87 H4
Luena, *Angola,* 104 C2
Luganville, *Vanuatu,* 55 N3
Lugo, *Spain,* 89 C6
Luhansk, *Ukraine,* 84 D4
Luiana, *Angola,* 104 D3
Lukulu, *Zambia,* 104 D2
Lumbala Kaquengue, *Angola,* 104 D2
Lumbala Nguimbo, *Angola,* 104 D2
Lundazi, *Zambia,* 105 F2
Lupilichi, *Mozambique,* 105 G2
Lusaka, *Zambia, national capital,* 104 E3
Lutsk, *Ukraine,* 87 H6
Luxembourg, *Europe, country,* 88 F4
Luxembourg, *Luxembourg, national*
  capital, 88 F4
Luxor, *Egypt,* 99 H3
Luzhou, *China,* 68 G5
Luzon, *Philippines,* 67 H4
Luzon Strait, *Philippines,* 67 H4
Lviv, *Ukraine,* 87 H6
Lyon, *France,* 89 F5
Lysychansk, *Ukraine,* 84 D4

m

Maan, *Jordan,* 73 C5
Maastricht, *Netherlands,* 88 F4
Macae, *Brazil,* 44 K4
Macapa, *Brazil,* 43 H3
Macau, *China,* 69 H6

Macedonia, *Europe, country,* 91 G3
Maceio, *Brazil,* 43 L5
Machakos, *Kenya,* 103 G4
Machala, *Ecuador,* 42 C4
Machu Picchu, *Peru,* 42 D6
Mackay, *Australia,* 55 J4
Mackenzie, *Canada,* 30 G2
Mackenzie Bay, *Canada,* 30 F2
Mackenzie Mountains, *Canada,* 30 F2
Macon, *U.S.A.,* 33 K4
Madagascar, *Africa, country,* 105 J4
Madang, *Papua New Guinea,* 54 K4
Madeira, *Atlantic Ocean,* 100 B2
Madeira, *Brazil,* 42 F5
Madingou, *Congo,* 102 B4
Madison, *U.S.A., internal capital,* 33 J2
Madras, *India,* 71 E8
Madrid, *Spain, national capital,* 89 D6
Madurai, *India,* 71 D9
Maevatanana, *Madagascar,* 105 J3
Mafeteng, *Lesotho,* 104 E5
Mafia Island, *Tanzania,* 103 H5
Magadan, *Russia,* 75 H3
Magangue, *Colombia,* 42 D2
Magdalena, *Bolivia,* 44 F2
Magdeburg, *Germany,* 88 G3
Magellan, Strait of, *South America,* 45 E10
Magnitogorsk, *Russia,* 85 H3
Mahajanga, *Madagascar,* 105 J3
Mahalapye, *Botswana,* 104 E4
Mahilyow, *Belarus,* 87 J5
Mahon, *Spain,* 89 F7
Maiduguri, *Nigeria,* 98 D6
Mai-Ndombe, Lake, *Democratic Republic*
  of Congo, 102 C4
Maine, *U.S.A., internal admin. area,*
  33 N1
Maine, Gulf of, *U.S.A.,* 33 N2
Maio, *Cape Verde,* 101 M11
Majorca, *Spain,* 89 E7
Majuro, *Marshall Islands, national capital,*
  52 E4
Makarikari, *Botswana,* 104 D4
Makassar Strait, *Indonesia,* 65 E4
Makeni, *Sierra Leone,* 101 C7
Makgadikgadi Pans, *Botswana,* 104 D4
Makhachkala, *Russia,* 72 E3
Makkovik, *Canada,* 31 P3
Makokou, *Gabon,* 102 B3
Makumbako, *Tanzania,* 103 F5
Makurdi, *Nigeria,* 102 A2
Mala, *Peru,* 42 C6
Malabo, *Equatorial Guinea,*
  national capital, 102 A3
Maladzyechna, *Belarus,* 87 H5
Malaga, *Spain,* 89 C7
Malaimbandy, *Madagascar,* 105 J4
Malakal, *Sudan,* 103 F2
Malakula, *Vanuatu,* 55 N3
Malang, *Indonesia,* 64 D5
Malanje, *Angola,* 104 C1
Malar, Lake, *Sweden,* 86 F4
Malatya, *Turkey,* 72 C2
Malawi, *Africa, country,* 105 F2
Malawi, Lake, *Africa,* 103 F6
Malaysia, *Asia, country,* 64 B2
Maldives, *Asia, country,* 71 C9
Male, *Maldives, national capital,* 71 C10
Malegaon, *India,* 71 C6
Mali, *Africa, country,* 100 E5
Malindi, *Kenya,* 103 H4
Malmo, *Sweden,* 87 E5
Malpelo Island, *Colombia,* 42 B3
Malta, *Europe, country,* 90 E4
Mamoudzou, *Mayotte,* 105 J2
Mamuno, *Botswana,* 104 D4
Man, *Ivory Coast,* 101 D7
Manado, *Indonesia,* 65 F3
Managua, *Nicaragua, national capital,*
  35 G5
Manakara, *Madagascar,* 105 J4
Manama, *Bahrain, national capital,* 73 F6
Manaus, *Brazil,* 43 G4
Manchester, *United Kingdom,* 88 D3
Manchuria, *China,* 69 K2
Mandalay, *Burma,* 66 C3

Mandera, *Kenya,* 103 H3
Mandritsara, *Madagascar,* 105 J3
Mandurah, *Australia,* 54 C6
Mangalore, *India,* 71 C8
Mania, *Madagascar,* 105 J3
Manicouagan Reservoir, *Canada,* 31 N3
Manila, *Philippines, national capital,*
  67 H5
Manisa, *Turkey,* 91 H4
Man, Isle of, *Europe,* 88 C3
Manitoba, *Canada, internal admin. area,*
  31 K3
Manitoba, Lake, *Canada,* 31 K3
Manizales, *Colombia,* 42 C2
Manja, *Madagascar,* 105 H4
Mannar, *Sri Lanka,* 71 E9
Mannar, Gulf of, *Asia,* 71 D9
Mannheim, *Germany,* 88 G4
Mansa, *Zambia,* 104 E2
Manta, *Ecuador,* 42 B4
Manzhouli, *China,* 75 F3
Mao, *Chad,* 98 E6
Maoke Range, *Indonesia,* 65 J4
Maputo, *Mozambique, national capital,*
  105 F5
Maraba, *Brazil,* 43 J5
Maracaibo, *Venezuela,* 42 D1
Maracaibo, Lake, *Venezuela,* 42 D2
Maracay, *Venezuela,* 42 E1
Maradi, *Niger,* 98 C6
Maranon, *Peru,* 42 C4
Marathon, *Canada,* 31 L4
Mar del Plata, *Argentina,* 45 G7
Margarita Island, *Venezuela,* 42 F1
Margherita Peak, *Africa,* 102 E3
Marib, *Yemen,* 73 E8
Maribor, *Slovenia,* 90 E2
Marie Byrd Land, *Antarctica,* 109 Q3
Mariental, *Namibia,* 104 C4
Marijampole, *Lithuania,* 87 G5
Marilia, *Brazil,* 44 J4
Marimba, *Angola,* 104 C1
Mariupol, *Ukraine,* 84 D4
Marka, *Somalia,* 103 H3
Marmara, Sea of, *Turkey,* 91 J3
Maroantsetra, *Madagascar,* 105 J3
Maroua, *Cameroon,* 102 B1
Marquesas Islands, *French Polynesia,*
  53 K5
Marrakech, *Morocco,* 100 D2
Marra, Mount, *Sudan,* 98 F6
Marsa Matruh, *Egypt,* 99 G2
Marseille, *France,* 89 F6
Marshall Islands, *Oceania, country,* 52 D3
Martapura, *Indonesia,* 64 D4
Martinique, *North America,* 34 M5
Mary, *Turkmenistan,* 72 H4
Maryland, *U.S.A., internal admin. area,*
  33 L3
Masaka, *Uganda,* 103 F4
Masasi, *Tanzania,* 103 G6
Masbate, *Philippines,* 67 H5
Maseru, *Lesotho, national capital,* 104 E5
Mashhad, *Iran,* 72 G4
Masirah Island, *Oman,* 73 G7
Massachusetts, *U.S.A.,*
  internal admin. area, 33 M2
Massangena, *Mozambique,* 105 F4
Massawa, *Eritrea,* 99 J5
Massif Central, *France,* 89 E5
Massinga, *Mozambique,* 105 G4
Masvingo, *Zimbabwe,* 104 F4
Matagalpa, *Nicaragua,* 35 G5
Matala, *Angola,* 104 B2
Matamoros, *Mexico,* 34 E2
Matanzas, *Cuba,* 35 H3
Mataram, *Indonesia,* 64 E5
Mataro, *Spain,* 89 E6
Matehuala, *Mexico,* 34 D3
Mato Grosso, Plateau of, *Brazil,* 43 G6
Maturin, *Venezuela,* 42 F2
Maui, *U.S.A.,* 33 P7
Maun, *Botswana,* 104 D3
Mauritania, *Africa, country,* 100 C5
Mauritius, *Indian Ocean, country,* 105 L3

Mavinga, *Angola,* 104 D3
Mayotte, *Africa,* 105 J2
Mazar-e Sharif, *Afghanistan,* 70 B3
Mazatlan, *Mexico,* 34 C3
Mazyr, *Belarus,* 87 J5
Mbabane, *Swaziland, national capital,*
  104 F5
Mbala, *Zambia,* 104 F1
Mbale, *Uganda,* 103 F3
Mbandaka, *Democratic Republic of*
  Congo, 102 C3
Mbarara, *Uganda,* 103 F4
Mbeya, *Tanzania,* 103 F5
Mbuji-Mayi, *Democratic Republic of*
  Congo, 102 D5
McClintock Channel, *Canada,* 30 J1
McClure Strait, *Canada,* 30 G1
McKinley, Mount, *U.S.A.,* 30 D2
Mead, Lake, *U.S.A.,* 32 D3
Mecca, *Saudi Arabia,* 73 C7
Mecula, *Mozambique,* 105 G2
Medan, *Indonesia,* 64 A3
Medellin, *Colombia,* 42 C2
Medford, *U.S.A.,* 32 B2
Medina, *Saudi Arabia,* 73 C7
Mediterranean Sea, *Africa/Europe,* 21
Medvezhyegorsk, *Russia,* 86 K3
Meerut, *India,* 70 D5
Meiktila, *Burma,* 66 C3
Meizhou, *China,* 69 J6
Mekele, *Ethiopia,* 103 G1
Meknes, *Morocco,* 100 D2
Mekong, *Asia,* 66 E5
Melaka, *Malaysia,* 64 B3
Melamo, Cape, *Mozambique,* 105 H2
Melanesia, *Oceania,* 52 D5
Melbourne, *Australia, internal capital,*
  54 H7
Melilla, *Africa,* 89 D7
Melitopol, *Ukraine,* 84 D4
Melo, *Uruguay,* 44 H6
Melville Island, *Australia,* 54 F2
Melville Island, *Canada,* 30 H1
Melville Peninsula, *Canada,* 31 L2
Memphis, *U.S.A.,* 33 J3
Mendoza, *Argentina,* 44 E6
Menongue, *Angola,* 104 C2
Mentawai Islands, *Indonesia,* 64 A4
Menzel Bourguiba, *Tunisia,* 98 C1
Mergui, *Burma,* 66 C5
Mergui Archipelago, *Burma,* 66 C5
Merida, *Mexico,* 34 G3
Meridian, *U.S.A.,* 33 J4
Merlo, *Argentina,* 44 E6
Mersin, *Turkey,* 72 B4
Meru, *Kenya,* 103 G3
Messina, *Italy,* 90 E4
Messina, *South Africa,* 104 F4
Metz, *France,* 88 F4
Mexicali, *Mexico,* 34 A1
Mexico, *North America, country,* 34 D3
Mexico City, *Mexico, national capital,*
  34 E4
Mexico, Gulf of, *North America,* 34 F3
Mexico, Plateau of, *Mexico,* 34 D2
Miami, *U.S.A.,* 33 K5
Michigan, *U.S.A., internal admin. area,*
  33 J2
Michigan, Lake, *U.S.A.,* 33 J2
Michurinsk, *Russia,* 84 E3
Micronesia, *Oceania,* 52 C4
Micronesia, Federated States of, *Oceania,*
  country, 52 C4
Middlesbrough, *United Kingdom,* 88 D3
Midway Islands, *Pacific Ocean,* 52 F2
Mikkeli, *Finland,* 86 H3
Milan, *Italy,* 90 D2
Milange, *Mozambique,* 105 G3
Mildura, *Australia,* 54 H6
Milwaukee, *U.S.A.,* 33 J2
Minas, *Uruguay,* 44 G6
Mindanao, *Philippines,* 67 H6
Mindelo, *Cape Verde,* 101 M11
Mindoro, *Philippines,* 67 H5
Mingacevir, *Azerbaijan,* 72 E3
Minna, *Nigeria,* 101 G7

ACKNOWLEDGEMENTS

Every effort has been made to trace the copyright holders of the material in this book. If any rights have been omitted, the publishers offer to rectify this in any subsequent edition, following notification. The publishers are grateful to the following organizations and individuals for their contributions and permission to reproduce material (t=top, m=middle, b=bottom, l=left, r=right):

Cover © Jacques Descloitres, MODIS Land Science Team; (globe) © Digital Vision; **Endpapers** © Ric Ergenbright/CORBIS; **p1** © Jim Zuckerman/CORBIS; **p2–3** © Art Wolfe/Science Photo Library; **p4–5** Stephen Moncrieff, Digital Vision; **p4** (tr) © Geospace/Science Photo Library; **p6** (bl) © CNES, 1988 Distribution SPOT Image/Science Photo Library; (mr) Stephen Moncrieff; **p7** (tm & tr) European Map Graphics Ltd; (b) © Paul A. Souders/CORBIS; **p8–9** (background) © Digital Vision; **p8** (mr) PHOTO ESA; **p9** (tl) © NERC Satellite Station, University of Dundee www.sat.dundee.ac.html; (br) Science Photo Library/European Space Agency; **p10** (b) Stephen Moncrieff; (tr) © Dan Guravich/CORBIS; **p11** (bl) European Map Graphics Ltd; (tr) © W. Perry Conway/CORBIS; **p12** (b) © Christopher Cormack/CORBIS; **p13** Stephen Moncrieff, Craig Asquith; **p14** (tr) © Bill Ross/CORBIS; (b) Craig Asquith; **p15** Craig Asquith; **p16–17** European Map Graphics Ltd; **p22–23** © Richard Cummins/CORBIS; **p23** (br) © W. Perry Conway/CORBIS; **p24** (tr) © Worldsat International/Science Photo Library; (m) © NASA/JSC; (b) © Raymond Gehman/CORBIS; **p25** © NASA/CORBIS; **p26–27** (b) © Richard Cummins/CORBIS; **p26** (t) © Dave G. Houser/CORBIS; **p27** (tr) © Joe McDonald/CORBIS; **p28** (l) © Angelo Hornak/CORBIS; (tr) © Carl & Ann Purcell/CORBIS; **p29** (tl) © Schafer & Hill/GettyImages; (br) © Michael & Patricia Fogden/CORBIS; **p36–37** © Galen Rowell/CORBIS; **p37** (tr) © Eye Ubiquitous/CORBIS; **p38** (m) © Julian Baum & David Angus/Science Photo Library; (bl) © Yann Arthus-Bertrand/CORBIS; (mr) © NASA/JSC; **p39** (r) © CNES, 1986 Distribution SPOT Image/Science Photo Library; (bl) © CNES, Distribution SPOT Image/Science Photo Library; **p40–41** (b) © Robert Frerck/GettyImages; **p40** (tr) Claus Meyer/GettyImages; **p41** (tl) Walter Bibikow/GettyImages; (tr) Peter Oxford/BBC Wild; **p46–47** © Still Pictures/Pascal Kobeh; **p47** (br) © Bates Littlehales/CORBIS; **p48–49** (b) © Amos Nachoum/CORBIS; **p48** (ml) © 1995, Worldsat International and J. Knighton/Science Photo Library; (tr) © NASA/JSC; **p49** (tr) © CNES, Distribution SPOT Image/Science Photo Library; (ml) © CORBIS; **p50** © Yoshio Tomii/Bruce Coleman; **p51** (tr) © Klein/Hubert/Still Pictures; (bl) © Zefa visual media; **p56–57** © Michael S. Yamashita/CORBIS; **p57** (br) © Keren Su/CORBIS; **p58** (tr) © Worldsat International/Science Photo Library; (m) © CNES, 1986 Distribution SPOT Image/Science Photo Library; (b) © Liu Liqun/CORBIS; **p59** (t) © NASA JPL; (br) © CNES, 1987 Distribution SPOT Image/Science Photo Library; **p60** (l) © Keren Su/CORBIS; (tr) © Keren Su/China Span/Alamy; **p61** (tl) © www.pictor.com; (b) © Papilio/CORBIS; **p62** (tr) © Richard T. Nowitz/CORBIS; (b) © Archivo Iconografico, S.A./CORBIS; **p63** (ml) © www.pictor.com; (tr) © Wolfgang Kaehler/CORBIS; (b) © Brian & Cherry Alexander Photography; **p76–77** © Digital Vision; **p77** (br) Agripicture/© Peter Dean; **p78–79** (b) © Peter Adams/GettyImages; **p78** (tr) NASA/GSFC/MITI/ERSDAC/JAROS, & U.S./Japan ASTER Science Team; (ml) © NASA GSFC Scientific Visualization Studio; **p79** (tr) © CNES, 1994 Distribution SPOT Image/Science Photo Library; (m) © German Remote Sensing Data Center; **p80** (tr) © The Art Archive/Historiska Muséet Stockholm/Dagli Orti; (bl) © Enzo & Paolo Ragazzini/CORBIS; **p81** (t) © Zefa visual media; (br) © Frans Lanting/Minden Pictures; **p82** © Paul Hardy/corbisstockmarket.com; **p83** (t) © Bob Krist/CORBIS; (b) © Araldo de Luca/CORBIS; **p92–93** © Tom Brakefield/CORBIS; **p93** (br) © Gallo Images/CORBIS; **p94** (tr) © Worldsat International/Science Photo Library; (bl) © Yann Arthus-Bertrand/CORBIS; (br) © NASA JPL; **p95** (r) © Jacques Descloitres, MODIS Land Science Team; (bl) © NASA/JSC; **p96** © Roger Wood/CORBIS; **p97** (ml) © Charles O'Rear/CORBIS; (tr) © Wolfgang Kaehler/CORBIS; (b) © Karl Ammann/CORBIS; **p106** (tr) © Worldsat International/Science Photo Library; (m) © Jan Jordan; **p107** (t) © NRSC Ltd/Science Photo Library; (b) © Digital Vision; **p110–111** (b) © Paul A. Souders/CORBIS; **p110** (tl) © Peter M. Wilson/CORBIS; (tm) © Joe McDonald/CORBIS; (ml) © Charles O'Rear/CORBIS; (mr) © Vanni Archive/CORBIS; **p111** (br) Galen Rowell/CORBIS; **p112–125** (background) © Digital Vision; (Afghanistan, Bahrain, Comoros, Rwanda, Turkmenistan and East Timor flags) © Shipmate Flags, Vlaardingen, The Netherlands; (all other flags) © Flag Enterprises Ltd; **p125** (b) AFP Photos/Henry Ray Abrams; **p126** (b) Craig Asquith.

Managing editor: Gillian Doherty
Managing designer: Mary Cartwright
Cover design by Zöe Wray
With thanks to Ruth King